The Lingerie
HANDBOOK

The *Lingerie* HANDBOOK

transform your body, 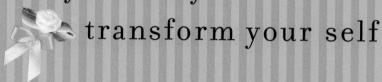 transform your self

Rebecca Apsan

WITH SARAH STARK

photographs by Jill Wachter
illustrations by Bunky Hurter

WORKMAN PUBLISHING • NEW YORK

To "the little flirt" in every woman

Library of Congress Cataloging-in-Publication information is available.
ISBN-13: 978-0-7611-4323-9; ISBN-10: 0-7611-4323-8

Designed by Janet Vicario

Workman books are available at special discounts when purchased in bulk
for premiums and sales promotions as well as for fund-raising or educational use.
Special editions also can be created to specification. For details, contact the
Special Sales Director at the address below.

WORKMAN PUBLISHING COMPANY, INC.
225 Varick Street
New York, NY 10014-4381
www.workman.com
www.thelittleflirt.com

Printed in U.S.A.

First printing: September 2006
10 9 8 7 6 5 4 3 2 1

❧ Contents ❧

*Guys: See pages 157–63!

Lingerie

French Dressing

BY CHARLES M. GREEN

It's the gift wrap on the present,
the garnish on the plate;
It's the exotic spice for that sweet vice
you love to contemplate.

It's the bottle that contains the wine,
the veil that hides the face;
It's the fog that shrouds the valley
in a mist of sheerest lace.

It's the pleasure in the morning
that you savor in the night;
It's those slinky satin secrets
you keep hidden for delight.

It's the subtle flash of stocking top
held tight by garter strap;
It's the slender strip of silk charmeuse
That baits the tender trap.

It's a way to tempt your lover
when you don't know what to say,
It's all this whispered in one word;
that word is . . . *lingerie.*

Stop Wearing Underwear!

❧ A Manifesto for Change ☙

*M*y name is Rebecca, and I am a lingerie enthusiast. Note, I'm not talking about underwear. I'm talking about lingerie—those pretty little underthings that are the first garments you put on in the morning, and the last ones you take off at night. Lingerie is so often underestimated. Considered frivolous. Condemned as steamy. And, worst of all, saved for special occasions.

But the right lingerie can do more than change your look, it can change your outlook. When you choose to wear your best bra and prettiest panties, you're preparing for a completely different kind of day than when you wear your saggiest and baggiest. Beyond making or breaking an outfit, lingerie has the ability to *transform,* allowing a woman to reinvent and revitalize herself, or simply to remember who she is.

That's why I've devoted my life to spreading the gospel of lingerie. And that's

Successful store windows are like a beautifully dressed woman: They reflect the personality— and the substance—of what lies inside.

why I named my store La Petite Coquette (that's French for "the Little Flirt"). I believe that everyone has a little flirt inside just waiting to be revealed. If your attitude toward undergarments is no frills, no thrills, think again. **Stop wearing underwear, and start wearing lingerie!**

Undergarments have been popping out of tops and peeping from pants for years, but in most circles intimate apparel remains somewhat of an unmentionable. Intimates are, by definition, private and personal. Yes, we see them everywhere, spread across advertisements, paraded across television screens, and plastered larger than life on

four-story billboards. And yet, after all that, people know very little about what lies beneath. I'd say that nine out of ten women who come to me for a fitting walk in wearing the wrong size bra. What you wear under there is an area of fashion that even the most fashionable neglect.

Women have been known to pop into my store and then spend the entire afternoon. It happens all the time. Why? Because when they walk in, it's as if they've entered an alternative universe, a candy store for grown-ups where silk robes stream from padded hangers in cascades of color and baskets overflow with soft, sumptuous fabrics and the lightest of lace. If it's their first time in this kind of environment, they are usually stunned at just how much they've been missing out on.

This ignorance about intimates is pandemic. All across the world, women who would never think of going outside in torn shirts or ripped pants have stashes of undergarments in sorry, stretched-out states—and probably in the wrong sizes too—that they consider perfectly suitable for wear. It's like cleaning the house before a guest arrives—we scramble and fuss to make sure we look good in the eyes of others, and end up stuffing things under the bed and inside the closets. Similarly, an outfit might look outwardly presentable, but it's sloppy just below the surface. And those bumps and bulges you're hiding might not be as invisible as you think! Lingerie is the complex layer of a woman that exists between her inside and the outside she shows to the world. It is the oft-overlooked middle area, the in-between. What's going on there? **And more important, how can we make it better?**

I understand that not everyone shares my aversion to bland, boring undergarments. "If it's not broken," they say, "it doesn't need to be fixed." *Au contraire!* As a bit of a provocateur, I challenge this complacency toward intimates daily. It is my mission to make women feel sexy, to bring out that fire they've long since forgotten or never knew they had in the first place. The way I see it, you only come around once in life, so you might as well have a good time.

In other words, if you don't expect a lot out of your underwear, you won't get very much from it. Exquisite lingerie is one of life's pleasures that, once experienced, is impossible to deny. The feel of luxurious fabrics against your skin helps you view the world through

different eyes. It's true! Whether I'm appearing on television or running everyday errands on my to-do list, I can't stop smiling if I've got something special on underneath. It's thrilling! If people ask me what occasion is appropriate for a particularly beautiful item, the answer is "Any time!" Someone once asked me, "Even when you're cleaning the kitchen floor?" *Especially* then—you might get very lucky!

Don't get me wrong, I'm a businesswoman, not a Pollyanna. I know that it's easy to feel stressed, less than enthusiastic, even invisible from time to time. But what I'm telling you is that lingerie can help counteract life's not-so-little negativities. It's so gratifying to me when I help a client try something she never would have considered and have her respond with, "Wow, it's amazing!" Or, I'll send a woman off in a new bra that looks beautiful, is actually comfortable, and makes her feel like she just dropped ten pounds. The transformation is remarkable. And it makes a difference.

Slip into something a little more comfortable.

Many people never get kudos in life, you know? They don't. Some have boring jobs, or they live alone. Some numb themselves to their sexuality. They are afraid of being intimate, and so hide themselves in unflattering underwear, rather than fortifying themselves with lovely lingerie. I make it a point to guide these women to find comfort within, to reawaken their sensuality and sometimes even their personality, to tease out their inner coquette. Lingerie is feminine armor. It's not made for battle or to defeat the world with brute force, but rather to softly protect and empower women against the hard breaks in life.

More amour: Valentine's Day windows at La Petite Coquette.

Lingerie is a big part of who I am. Not only because I work in the lingerie business or wear the actual garments (you bet I do!), but because it defines my approach to life. Lingerie is more than a bit of lace or a sliver of satin. It's about the small ways we spice things up and make our worlds a little better. I like to surround myself with a beautiful environment—soft lighting, great music, a sweet scent . . . my ways of creating a pleasurable existence. If this sounds like it's coming from a lady who lives a life of leisure, someone who has too much time on her hands, it's exactly the opposite.

Transformation Begins at Home

I am a working woman who has spent the past thirty years building a business and an identity in a store that started out the size of a closet. I'm a big believer in transformation—after all, that is how La Petite Coquette was born in the first place. I opened my own business because my husband at the time lent me some money to get me out of his hair. Little do my customers know that the original space, which is just across the street from my current location, was once a kosher barbecue chicken joint, where the owner killed fresh chickens and roasted them on a grill right in the window. (Everyone said it was the best chicken they'd ever eaten.) The place was filthy when I moved in—the grease and sawdust covering the floor were the least of the mess. Well, I got in there and turned it into one of the hottest lingerie destinations in New York City, stuffing more merchandise than you can believe into those 160 square feet. It's hard to imagine that my tiny jewelry box of a store was hatched from such squalor! From roasting chickens to hot chicks? Anything is possible.

1980: Starting out, I had a small store, some good friends (that's Janie holding Chloe), and a very big dream.

Everybody has something special in herself, even if she doesn't recognize it at first. I apply this same logic to lingerie. If you feel like you've got nothing going on, a little silk will create a whole new scenario in your mind. If a woman feels embarrassed about her body, she needs only to learn the things that will look best on her and she will shine. Or if she feels like her relationship is a little dull, I encourage her to open up and try something different. If you don't ask for what you want, and then make some effort to pursue it, you'll never be happy.

How do I know all this? Because I've spent the better part of my life behind the dressing room curtain where, once their clothes start to come off, women begin to reveal themselves. No, not just private parts, I'm talking private lives. In five minutes they begin to talk about the most

Here I am today, presiding over my palace of pretty things.

personal of topics, the things they've never told anybody else. It's scary for people to take their clothes off, but once they do, the emotional shields come down as well. In these unusual circumstances, I often feel like a therapist—listening, comforting, encouraging, advising, and sharing myself with these women who, in the end, are not so different from me. It's quite remarkable how similar we all are in our insecurities, regardless of age, body, bank account, or boyfriend status.

Speaking of therapists, I love the fact that my shop happens to be located in an area of New York City I like to call "therapists' row." I get both the anxious ladies who come into my store before their sessions and the ones who come in glassy-eyed afterward. Not to mention the therapists themselves—some of my best customers! Lingerie is an indulgence women treat themselves to when they're feeling down because, like cosmetics, it gives instant gratification. On other occasions, women buy lingerie for the reason most commonly expected—seduction. When they're starting a relationship, they have a rejuvenated interest in looking their best. Suddenly, they remember to tap into their feminine toolbox and start wearing the pretty, frilly things that have spent too much time at the back of the drawer.

Speaking of Men . . .

Although every once in a long while you'll come across a man who says that lingerie does little for him, most love it. It has played a big part in my own relationships. My ex-husband used to literally rip it off my body in the heat of the moment. That behavior became an expensive habit—which was another motive for me to open a shop of my own! **Lingerie is beautiful, but it's also symbolic—**it calls attention to the very area it covers up. It hints at, but does not reveal, what is hidden underneath. It lets you show off . . . yet only so much. It's the ultimate tease. There's a lot of mystery involved in lingerie—and I like to keep it that way, leaving something to the imagination. It's so much more seductive to let a little lace peek out here or there, than to have everything hanging out. A boyfriend once said it perfectly when he told me, "Lingerie is like the curtain that separates the audience from the performance."

Part of the allure is that lingerie is quintessentially female. Men don't wear lingerie; they wear boxers or briefs. (Or maybe boxer briefs if they're really stretching their imaginations.) On the other hand, lingerie has multiple levels of meaning. It is both practical (providing protection for the body and shape under clothing) and sexual (highlighting physical assets and desirability). But its implications are also, on a larger stage,

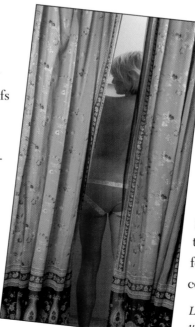

both political and social. Trends in lingerie parallel the way society sees women, and the way they see themselves. It's no coincidence that when the birth control pill came out, women embraced their newfound sexual freedom by abandoning the restrictive girdles and garters of their mothers. Even the most functional purposes for wearing a push-up bra or a control garment are linked to

Lingerie is a sneak preview, not the whole show.

society's view of the ideal female form at any given moment. Can you imagine if male status was reflected in their personal choices (and the choices available) of underwear?

Sure, a man can choose to wear a thong or leopard bikini, but even the tightiest of tightie-whities says little about how a man stacks up. But lingerie does everything to express the woman who wears it. The colors alone have associations: White is pure and innocent, black is sophisticated and seductive, red is sultry and sexy, pastels and florals are pretty and sweet, animal prints are wild. What does a man's choice in the stripes or checks on his boxer shorts communicate about his state of mind?

While there is nothing wrong with wanting to look irresistible to men, why wait around in ugly underwear until a guy comes your way? Why not strut your stuff, man or no man? (And, by the way—for you gals who like gals, this goes for you too. Throughout the book, when I talk

Innocent

Sophisticated

Sexual

Sweet

Wild

about men, I urge you to mentally edit and substitute the gender-specific words that work for you.)

It's no accident that lingerie items are also known as "foundation garments." That's exactly what they are—the layers worn closest to the body as a base for outerwear, and the secret support system that sometimes follows, sometimes creates, but always mirrors who you are and how you feel.

Lingerie is like an internal smile. Even if nobody sees what's actually underneath, the impression radiates to the outside and draws others to you. Everybody loves confidence. And despite what most people think, lingerie is much more about wits and sass than . . . well, you know how to rhyme. **This attitude is the essence of a true coquette.** Always remember: To adorn yourself is to adore yourself. And even when you don't feel so hot, or things aren't going so hot, there are always hot pants!

Launch the New You

One of the reasons people like to shop at my store is because of the honesty. In addition to a comfortable environment, they receive expert advice that is forthright. Customers trust that they're not going to get an "Oh, yeah, it fits you well" from me, or any of my staff. I'm more likely to say "Take it off!" Then I'll bring something else, asking sweetly, "Why don't you try this?"

I know that not everyone can make it to my shop, but with this book, you have everything you need to know about the state of undress—and underdress. **This flirt-in-training manual will take you through all the assorted little somethings to help you change your life, your looks . . . and maybe your luck.** Just like I do with my customers, we'll start by finding you a bra that finally fits and go from there. You'll get the lowdown on panties. The secrets of shapewear. Some highlights of hosiery. Discover the things that make men break out into a sweat when they come to the store. Learn how to make lingerie last— and when to say good-bye. These tips and tricks are not just for movie stars and models, but for mere mortals too.

I've had many first-time lingerie customers walk out of my store as converts, thrilled to leave in comfort and confidence. I'll show you how to get that feeling; I'll take you there and lay it bare. I hope that you walk away from these lessons in lingerie feeling sexy, strong, and ready to say "Okay, world, here I am."

BARE TRUTH

The origin of the word *lingerie* comes from the French word *linge*, referring to linens. Bedclothes and undergarments were once made out of the same fabrics, with the same techniques and embellishments, and were often laundered together. Indeed, for the underclass of certain periods, underwear was often made out of old bedsheets that had become worn and soft. What one wore under the covers evolved into what one wore under clothing. A woman often slept in her camisoles and chemises, which served double-duty by being the thin protective liner under stiff and scratchy corsets, bustles, hoops, and dresses.

It's What's Inside That Counts

Getting to Know Your Inner Flirt

Through the years, there are no four words I've heard as frequently as *you changed my life*. The women I've fitted are amazed by their underwear awakenings, shocked at the power of lingerie, and thankful for the opportunity to start anew. Lingerie is one of the few things in life that really works magic—and instantly.

The sad thing is that a lot of women don't think they're worthy of nice lingerie—or that nice lingerie is worth the money. While they're willing to spend cash on their outer clothing, they feel guilty buying something intended for a few eyes only. To some women, lingerie is impractical. They say, "Oh, who cares? Who's going to see it?" I say it's what's on the inside that counts. Even if you're the only one who knows, so what? You're the one who matters. What women don't always realize is that even if others can't see the undergarments, the effect they create is not lost. Far from it. When you wear gorgeous lingerie, you walk differently, you think differently, and you are perceived differently.

Intimacy Issues

O ne thing I've learned in all my years dealing with half-naked females is that most women aren't happy with the way they look. No matter what, there's always something that makes us feel inadequate—we're not thin enough, attractive enough, smart enough, rich enough, loved enough. Such image and self-esteem issues keep us from feeling positive about ourselves—or only feeling good when we get complimented or praised by someone else. When you buy lingerie that makes *you* feel better, you start to take life by the horns. No more sitting there like a lady-in-waiting, hoping that somebody will come by, scoop you up, and whisk you off to the life you always dreamed about. And though lingerie may seem like a frivolous indulgence to some, it's actually a realistic way to take control of your life and happiness. Buying the right lingerie is no small, insignificant step. After all, it's not superficial to address the very issues that eat away at you. In that regard, lingerie is cheaper than therapy. And as far as I'm concerned, lingerie *is* therapy.

> **Though lingerie may seem like a frivolous indulgence to some, it's actually a realistic way to take control of your own happiness.**

BETTER PACKAGING

A s for your actual body, lingerie can physically transform it, immediately. Let's face it, no matter how you looked ten years ago or plan to look in ten months, right now you look the way you look. It's not so easy to change your body, but you can easily update packaging.

A lot of women believe they have to have the body of a lingerie model to warrant owning an underwear drawer full of beautiful things. They're afraid they might not look good enough in lingerie. This is especially true for the curvy girls (which is my term for women with fuller bodies—I find the term *plus-size* offensive and would never want to be called that myself). **I've had curvy girls in my shop literally cry with joy** when they find a bra or other piece of lingerie that fits them properly— **and even looks dainty, not matronly.** I've bumped into customers at restaurants and they've brought me to meet their friends—they've even flashed me! And I've

Behind-the-seams secrets of starlet style.

witnessed smaller-chested girls see their reflections in the dressing room mirror and scream, "Oh. My. God. I have boobs!" After a lifetime of feeling like misfits because of mis-fits, many believe that nothing is meant for their bodies and everything looks bad on them. The styles and shapes they want are not made or readily available, so they stop trying. I'm here to say, don't give up!

I can't blame the woman who feels she's been burned in the past or is too intimidated to look for lingerie because her body does or doesn't look a certain way. We all hold ourselves to impossibly high standards. I love lingerie more than, well, most anyone, but I have plenty of things I'd like to change about my own body. This might surprise a lot of people because I'm very bold with my lingerie, but at some point you have to get over your insecurities. I certainly don't let mine stop me. Personally, wearing lingerie has made me appreciate different aspects of my body, instead of focusing on the parts I'd rather forget about. Let me take that back; it does let me forget about them—at least temporarily!

With lingerie, nothing is set in skin and bones. **Why focus on what you cannot fix when there are so many ways to amplify, accentuate, and emphasize what you've got?** And you can even change it on a daily basis. Lingerie brings out the best. It can hide, distract from, or downplay any imperfection. Some garments are actually designed to do just that. The right bra can make a woman look like she's lost fifteen pounds or boost small breasts into eye-catching décolleté. Pairing pants or a skirt with the proper panties guarantees the end of visible panty lines (VPL). Those ridges and ripples created by the elastic bands on most panties are an evil that is far from necessary. Shapewear can give you what Mother Nature did not: a flatter stomach and thighs that look as free from cellulite as a twelve-year-old's. Did I mention the

The right undergarments make the outfit.

possibilities of the perfectly proportioned curves of a movie star on the red carpet? (You better believe she's thankful for the control undergarments that create this illusion!) Stockings upgrade your legs the way lipstick highlights a kissable pout. Underneath the lingerie, it's still you, only better. In this age of enhancement, implants, injections, and extreme makeovers, lingerie increases the sexiness without the surgery.

Some types of lingerie may not reshape your body, but are so beautiful they outshine anything you might be worried about. I call it the lingerie mystique—that hidden intrigue that creates the allure. This is

where the seductive element of lingerie really comes forth. I guarantee that you can blind a lover to your flaws by wearing certain undergarments. Trust me, with that silky blue chemise enveloping your body, the last thing he'll be noticing is your cellulite. But I'm less concerned with pleasing him, and more with helping you enjoy yourself. If you're happy and into it, he'll vicariously reap the benefits.

Listen to me: We've all been known to position ourselves so that we're seen at our best angle. But all this self-consciousness detracts from the moment. **Lingerie is a visual trick that draws attention to the places you want to be seen, and away from those you'd prefer to hide.** Worried about a bulging belly? A babydoll, slip, or floaty camisole diverts attention from your stomach. Don't feel so good about your derriere? A thong or lacy panty is a distracting invitation to a party that a lover can only hope he'll be invited to attend. Lingerie is an embellishment, a flag of femininity that calls attention to itself. The benefit? *You can relax.* It conceals as much as it reveals, and the varying degrees of exposure are entirely up to you. But remember this: It takes more nerve to be naked than to wear a negligee!

Think Yourself Beautiful

*B*ut assuming lingerie is just about sex is like thinking clothing is just about fashion. It's far more complicated. In fact, the sexiness isn't in the lingerie itself, but in the woman wearing it. No matter how you feel about your body, when you present it in a way that you think is the most beautiful, you're a stunner. You feel alive—and others can sense that quality in you. It's true. Everyone has had those moments when she's felt *on*—those days when you carry a little spark and people take notice. Lingerie helps create that mood; it helps make those "on" moments happen. It reminds you that you're looking good, that you are worthy of being worshipped, appreciated, and loved. I know all this might sound superficial or trite, but treating yourself to some lingerie is a way of improving your life that many women deny themselves. And as far as I can see, it is the easiest self-help program I've come across.

> No matter how you feel about your body, when you present it in a way that you think is beautiful, you're a stunner.

As I mentioned before, this is about seducing yourself—or at least seeing yourself as being worthy of seduction. Why should he get treated to the delicate black lace on a date, while you get the granny panties on a night home alone? Don't store your sexiness on a shelf, waiting for the day someone reaches up to pull it out for you. If you freeze life because you're waiting for something, you can all too easily get stuck in a rut. As they say, objects in motion tend to stay in motion.

If it seems like I attribute too much importance to lingerie, that I overestimate its capacity to work wonders, it's only because of the many women who have told me how lingerie has changed their lives. Women who have found a little glamour, even as they sit under the fluorescent lights of a conference room, or drive kids to school, or schlep to the store.

I'm always so happy to hear that I've helped someone, whether because of the lingerie itself, or the new mind-set that comes from wearing it. My views may not seem so strange once you experience the transformation yourself. As your faithful guide to the fine art of flirtdom, I'd like to start with you.

The Little Flirt

WHERE'S YOURS?

hen a woman says to me, "I'm not the type for lingerie," I say, "There is no type." Because, put simply, my philosophy is, *Dress in a way that would make someone want to undress you.* Even if that someone exists only in your imagination. I mean it. Rather than hiding yourself, take what you've got and work it. The excuse that it's not your thing just doesn't work with me; there are simply too many styles to choose from.

> **Rather than hiding yourself, take what you've got and work it.**

Lots of women's magazines have little quizzes and charts that claim to reveal your personal style. While such formulas might apply to regular clothing, I don't buy any of them when it comes to lingerie. Lingerie is more about mood and occasion. Does the circumstance warrant sophisticated, sultry, or sweet? It depends on what you feel like at any given moment. People are always curious about the women who wear various types of lingerie. They want to know who actually buys the racy items that make the average shopper blush. Well, it could be anyone. I've also been asked on occasion to speculate about the kind of lingerie a certain woman is wearing. The truth is, you never can tell. There is no direct correlation between a woman's panties and her person-

ality or outward appearance. She might have a specific style that she thinks is more "her," but there's plenty of crossover. **A preppy woman isn't necessarily going to wear basic white cotton briefs with her plaids and penny loafers.** You can't judge a book by its cover. The pages inside (or the panties underneath!) can be entirely different from the jacket. In my experience, most women wear a mix.

The majority of us are attracted to many different styles of clothes—which may explain those purchases that live, tags still attached, deep in the closet. It's harder to deviate much from your general style in outward dressing than it is in "under" dressing. When you wear lingerie you have one of two scenarios: Either nobody will see you, letting you safely play out your fantasies and fetishes, or you'll show that side of you to a person of your choosing. It's a more private way to indulge your many fashion facets.

Some of the women who come into my store—the doctors, lawyers, and professors —are ones you'd expect might be more conservative. As I said before: not necessarily. These powerful, successful women are wearing sexy stuff underneath those suits! Because they often have to desexualize themselves outwardly in order to be respected in the workplace, they like to soften up what they wear underneath. It's their way of feeling feminine—an attribute whose concealment is, unfortunately, sometimes a better career move. Here's an extreme example, but she was one of my favorite clients—a judge who bought crotchless panties. I just love the image of her sitting on the bench wearing the black robe with her air-conditioned underwear underneath!

The point is, lingerie is meant to make you feel fabulous, however you define it. A black lace bra is equally appropriate on a twenty-year-old in tight jeans as it is on a seventy-year-old in a sweater set. Sure, some styles are younger and trendier, with sassy sayings and funky prints, but those are only a few. For the most part, once puberty is behind you, there's no need to worry that lingerie isn't meant for someone your age. Anything goes!

And it's never too late to start. Even if you've been doing it wrong all along, you can recover quickly, easily, and enjoyably. Unlike other transformations that might require grueling effort and countless hours at the gym (or in the therapist's office), a complete overhaul of your underthings can be achieved in a single weekend. Instant gratification, for both body and brain! Get ready to take the first step in turning around your lingerie life.

Kiss lackluster lingerie goodbye!

Address Your State of Undress

The transformation begins with an assessment of your current inventory of intimates. Are your underwear drawers overflowing, yet you often find yourself with nothing to wear? A drawer stuffed with things—full of possibility, or so you think—can easily trick you into thinking you have everything you need. You might ask yourself, "How can I justify buying more when I already have so much?" Or, "Why buy another demi bra when I don't wear the one I have?" Not to get too philosophical, but the answer is in the question. Maybe you don't wear the things you have because something is wrong with them. Simply put, quantity does not equal quality. Do not be deceived by an excess of surplus goods.

> **Are your underwear drawers overflowing, yet you often find yourself with nothing to wear?**

YOUR FIRST TASK

Take all your lingerie and spread it out on the bed. Why? Because your personal stash probably needs some pruning. It's impossible to evaluate all your goods if you can't see everything. Separate into categories. Sort bras and panties by style, then by occasion (everyday or fancy), and, finally, by color. Classify every last thing, one thong at a time.

Editing lingerie is easier than regular clothing because usually you only have to determine between things to keep and things to toss. There should be no maybes. No save-for-another-seasons. None of those but-it-might-come-back-in-styles.

LET GO

Time to pare down. Ditch anything you wouldn't want to be seen wearing. And start inspecting what remains. Say sayonara if:

❀ **It's discolored or faded.** Has bright white become dingy gray? Is a much-loved item past its prime and ready to retire?

❀ **The elastic is going—or gone.** Just because something is not seen by others is no reason it should still be worn. If it's lost its original shape, toss it.

❀ **It's worn out, frayed, or threadbare.** Into the waste bin it goes. Do you think tattered lingerie is like a child's security blanket? Let it go.

THE 3 *F*s

*A*sk the following three questions of every piece of lingerie you own. If you can't answer yes to all three, don't let that bra or panty take up space in your drawer.

Fit: Is it right for my body and my lifestyle?

Flatter: Does it make me look good and enhance what I've got?

Feel: Does it feel good on my body and do I feel great wearing it?

❁ **The underwires are distorted, or even poking dangerously through fabric.** No further explanation necessary, I hope.

❁ **It hasn't been worn in over a year.** There must be a reason. Was it buried—out of sight, out of mind? Or is it not an everyday item, something that should go into storage? Anything you haven't touched in six months should be tried on and reassessed.

❁ **It doesn't fit properly anymore.** Weight fluctuates. Women hang on to bras, especially expensive ones, waiting for their body to return to an earlier incarnation. This happens frequently with women who were recently pregnant. Even if they eventually end up at their former size, their shape sometimes has changed. Stop holding out for the day you lose a lot of weight or dramatically change your body. Buy new things when that time actually comes—that's when you'll deserve a reward anyway!

❁ **It didn't fit properly to begin with.** We've all bought garments out of desperation, like the time you bought a slip in the wrong size because there were no others to go under a sheer dress you were wearing to a wedding that started in five hours! Or, we've bought something because we really, really wanted the item and were lured by its siren song, despite the fact that it just didn't fit. If it's the wrong size, or wrong for your body type, it's got to go.

❁ **It's uncomfortable.** Free yourself of anything that feels bad, even if it looks good. Bras that dig in. Thongs that ride up. Slips that pucker and pull. There is a limit to how much one should suffer for beauty.

❁ **It's almost the perfect thing.** While surveying the situation, you might find you've duplicated a lot of items on past shopping trips. Most of us are attracted

GOOD BRAS GONE BAD

*W*hile this is an exception to the rule, some bras *can* be fixed. If the fit is otherwise perfect, you can sometimes bring a bra back to life.

Problem	Solution
The band is a little tight	Bra extenders, available at better boutiques and notions stores, will lengthen the band.
The band is too loose	Some lingerie stores have seamstresses on hand to take in the band; otherwise, take the bra to any seamstress or tailor.
The straps fall down	While you should consider wearing a tighter band size (more on that later), you can invest in some Strap-Mates, which can help stop slippage. When your straps slip, it's usually a sign of narrow shoulders and a narrow rib cage. (Read the next chapter for more on proper fit.)
The straps dig into your shoulders	Strap cushions can increase comfort. If the straps still dig, pitch the bra and consider going up a cup size and down a band size.
The hooks are broken or mangled	Hooks can be replaced by sewing on new ones. An easy way to lengthen the life of a beloved bra!

to certain features or styles and end up buying the same things over and over. You know that friend of yours who dates the "same" person over and over again, who repeats the same dynamic in every relationship, with a template man with characteristics identical to the last? That's exactly how a lot of us shop. Do you have piles of bikinis, but only one full-coverage brief? Are all your underthings in varying shades of white? Do you have fifteen bras, but not one with straps that hide under tank tops? **Bras can be like the perfect black pants—you can own countless pairs, but still not have found The One. If you don't love it, lose it.**

EXCUSES, EXCUSES, EXCUSES

I will grant three exceptions to the rules of trash-can death for lingerie that really should go—but don't try to apply them too frequently.

GIVEAWAYS. This is for all you lingerie lovers out there. If you are guilty of possessing items that have lived a long career in the back of your drawer or that you hardly ever wore, you might consider passing your neglected negligee on to charity, a relative, or a friend. While some women might feel there's a stigma attached to receiving intimate apparel hand-me-downs, **there are others who scan antiques stores and flea markets to pick up such vintage treasures.** I've shared the wealth of my rarely worns with plenty of friends and family members. At the risk of sounding indelicate, make sure your castoffs are in pristine condition. Send anything that's not to the trash heap.

TUNE-UPS. Some garments may require only a little maintenance to be wearable again. This happens infrequently because lingerie, by its very nature, is delicate. Once it starts to fall apart, it is rarely salvageable. A tailor can, however, recover some items with open seams, loosened hems, or broken clasps. (See "Good Bras Gone Bad," opposite.)

SENTIMENTAL VALUE. By all means, keep anything to which you have a strong emotional attachment—a slip that belonged to your mother or a present from your husband when he was still your boyfriend. Just make sure your entire stash is not a walk down memory lane, a relic from the past never to be used again. Lingerie is meant to be worn!

MOVING ON

Now that you've said some good-byes, you can move on to making good buys! Stick with me and I guarantee these lessons in lingerie will tap into the little flirt within you.

Breast Interests

Bras

The right bra is like the perfect man: good-looking, supportive, and sure never to let you down. It's also just as hard to find.

In the lingerie business, it's common knowledge that the majority of women wear their bras in the wrong size. Ask around and you'll hear percentages ranging from 70 to 85 percent. Whatever the exact numbers, the takeaway is that most women don't feel as comfortable or look as good as they could. True, you may be among the minority that has it right, but it's

worth double-checking. The wrong bra can make you look fat . . . or totally flat. It can make a young woman look dumpy and beyond her years. The right bra can give a fifty-five-year-old woman the bust of a thirty-year-old and will do more for her appearance than all the antiwrinkle creams in the world.

So why, given all the money and energy we pour into our looks, do some women still consider it an indulgence to invest in a good bra? I mean, what sounds more frivolous than bra shopping? Purchasing a bra might give the same rush of excitement you get from buying other typically female things, like a new pair of heels or even a daring shade of lipstick, but it truly is an investment, and in most cases a necessity. More than any other article of lingerie, the right bra can dramatically alter your appearance, improve your comfort level, and change your outlook—the way you carry yourself, the way you are perceived, even the way you think. It sounds impossible, but it's true: **The right bra** has the power to transform you.

But finding the right bra isn't easy. You know the scenario: You walk into a department store or lingerie shop, wander around the racks looking for the same size you wore when you were eighteen. You pick up a few bras in that size, try them on, noticing the pinching feeling in the band, the pressing of the underwire, or the gaping in the cups. None seems to fit quite right, so you make another round through the store. By the time you're done, you've been there so long you can feel the salesperson thinking, "What is this woman doing?" You don't want to leave empty-handed, so you buy the bra that seems like the best of the bunch. Guess what? Bad idea.

Look, I know that the actual experience of bra shopping is infamously difficult, a groan-inducing chore often dreaded as much as getting waxed. If you shop mainly at department stores, you have to wade through cluttered racks where merchandise is jammed together, categorized by brand rather than by purpose, with little attention to style, sizing, or color. The atmosphere is uninviting, and if there are any identifiable salespeople, they keep themselves busy avoiding the bewildered look in your eye. You wonder if they are intentionally ignoring you as you try to separate a bra that won't let go of the tangled straps and clear plastic hangers that surround it. Discount stores are even tougher to negotiate. Sure, the prices may be right, but limits on how many items you can bring into the dressing room are a drag—and sometimes you can't even try on lingerie. Attracted by a good deal, you end up with three bras that never feel right.

It's exhausting. But don't lose hope: I've got lots of tricks that will make it easier to navigate around the land mines of lingerie sections.

The perfect pick-me-up.

Accepting the Challenge

It's important to understand the complexities of bra fit, rather than settling because we blame ourselves for not sizing up in some way or another. Our bodies change over time, and sometimes week by week. That's the first challenge. One of the areas where weight fluctuation is most evident is our breasts. Indeed, the average woman will wear several different bra sizes throughout her life. How long has it been since you've checked yours? Have *you* worn the same size since you stopped growing? Ever go on the birth control pill . . . off the pill . . . had a child . . . breast-fed? Does your weight fluctuate according to your menstrual cycle? Have all those mornings at the gym begun to pay off, or are you starting to see the effects of not working out? Has gravity caused your boobs to look down instead of straight ahead? Do you find that you want to rip off your bra at the end of the day? If you answered yes to any—yes, ANY—of these questions, you probably need to reexamine both your mind-set and your bra size.

> **Introducing yourself to lingerie is an education. And when it comes to bras, most of us are still in the dark ages.**

What I'd like you to do first is to think of your bra not as a pretty fluff piece, but as a work of careful engineering. And the bigger your breasts are, the more complicated the "rigging"—and not just by a little, but by a lot. The worst part about all this is that most women accept bra discomfort unquestioningly, assuming that it's just one of those things. No matter what size you are, bras are meant to help, not hinder. Yet people look at me like I'm joking when I say that a bra should be comfortable!

Women who are really into fashion don't necessarily know more about proper bra fit than the most clueless, couldn't-care-less cases. You'd think that someone who reads every magazine would have a better shot at understanding how bra sizing works—but they don't! The playing field is level in this regard. The few-and-far-between who are more knowledgeable in this department usually have a specific person or experience that they can credit for their bra-awareness. Maybe your grandmother took you to a department store where you got the kind of service you just don't get anymore, or maybe you went to a professional fitter and realized you're a completely different size than you thought. But if I have any say in the matter, all women will get bra savvy. We all have our dreams. Mine is that in ten years we'll look back in disbelief that almost every woman experienced some sort of breast or bra discomfort daily.

THE FIRST HURDLE

Okay, time to face the music . . . or the mirror. Many, many women buy the bra size they want to be rather than the one that fits. It's psychological— we convince ourselves that we are a certain size, and we

Mirror, mirror . . .

cling to it for dear life. Now, I know we don't always want to accept that we've gained weight or that our bodies aren't what they used to be. To acknowledge that is to admit the passage of time. One of my store regulars told me that she used to pride herself on having breasts like wineglasses turned up to the sky, but now they are more like champagne flutes hanging down. But trust me on this: Nobody is going to know if you've gone from a 32C to a 34D. What they *can* tell is if you're not fitting in your clothing. This is where you need to free your mind. Like it or not, love it or hate it, your body is the size it

is, regardless of the numbers and letters. Stuffing your size nine foot into a size seven shoe is not going to make your foot look smaller—it's going to look ridiculous, not to mention hurt like hell! Likewise, wearing a bra that is too small will not make your breasts any smaller. And if your breasts have shrunk from weight loss, breast-feeding, or going off the pill, the bra you wore when your breasts were bigger won't support or maximize your current assets.

BARE FACT

We adopted the word *brassiere,* unsurprisingly, from France (where it is an obsolete term for "bodice"). What may surprise you is that the French don't say "brassiere" or "bra," but *soutien-gorge*—which means throat support. Think about that one for a moment!

UNDERSTANDING BRAS

While some fit problems stem from your ever-changing body, others have more to do with the bra itself, complicated endlessly by industry sizing issues, plus the all-important variables of style, fabric,

If you've tried bra shopping on your own and still can't find the one you love, it may be time to call in the professionals. Just think of a bra specialist as a dating service for your breasts. In half the time and with better results, a professional fitter can guide you to the bra that's just right for you. Unfortunately, many women are uncomfortable talking about their breasts and cringe at the thought of showing a salesperson how they look in a bra. They might imagine getting manhandled by fusty, matronly ladies (who, by the way, probably know their stuff). But you have to understand that salespeople who are accustomed to fitting women for bras are extremely professional. They do this every day. They understand when customers are shy and try their best to make everyone feel comfortable. In lingerie and in life, some things are hard to ask for, but if you don't put yourself out there, you'll never get what you want.

MAMMARY MYSTERIES

Though most scientists believe that our natural breast support comes from rubbery Cooper's ligaments that lace through the breasts, others claim that skin plays a bigger supporting role. One thing is for certain: Breasts contain no muscle. None. Yes, there may be muscle behind your breasts, but the truth is, there is nothing you can do (apart from augmentation) to stop the downward slide of your breasts except wear a good bra.

elasticity, and personal fit preferences. Just as no two women are alike, neither are any two bras alike. Even if you fill out a 34C demi cup bra beautifully, you might be swimming in a 34C full coverage bra. Bra sizing is much more than just a numbers game.

If only bra fit were a science, or something women intuitively knew how to do (or learned from their mothers), something like putting on mascara or braiding hair! But bras don't work that way, in part because they're always changing. The bras I sold thirty years ago are entirely different from the bras I sell today—and forget about the bras that were sold thirty years before then. To begin with, innovations in fabric have brought us man-made fibers that fit better, feel more comfortable, and breathe like 100 percent cotton. The ideal breast shape has also changed; these days most women want their boobs to look like boobs—not torpedoes or boyish pancakes. Then there's us—we are a very differently shaped population than our mothers' generation. Yes, we weigh more. Factor in fewer knowledgeable salespeople . . . well, the challenge is huge.

Every woman knows how it feels to go on a million dates before finding the right man. The same is true for bras. It takes time and patience in a fitting room, and the willingness to go home without getting lucky. But you'll never find the perfect someone if you don't look. So, let's get ready to shop.

hot dates for bras

Ancient Greece

✿ **Bra Beginnings**

Women in ancient Greece bind their breasts with a piece of cloth or a leather strip—a *strophium*—but, interestingly, wear it *over* their tunics.

1500s

✿ **Scent of a Woman**

To perfume their rarely washed clothing, ladies wear a scented pomander or sachet between the breasts, a reminder of which is seen today in the embroidered rosette at the center of some bras.

1863 ▼

✿ **Start of Support**

The first patent for a breast supporter, which was designed as an alternative to the corset, is issued to Luman L. Chapman.

1889

✿ **Bra du Jour**

Herminie Cadolle, founder of the famous French company Cadolle, is often credited with creating the bra. She displayed an early version at the 1889 Paris Exposition. Called the *bien-être*, or "well-being," it is still attached to a corset in the back, but is the first undergarment to present the revolutionary concept of supporting the breasts from above, rather than from below.

1904–1905

✿ **Bonjour Brassieres**

The term *brassiere* is introduced in the United States but refers to something more resembling a camisole stiffened with boning than a modern bra. Until the mid-1930s, the full word *brassiere* appears in ads, though the word *bra* is part of the vernacular.

1914

✿ **Debutante's Debut**

With the help of her maid, New York socialite Mary Phelps Jacob (who later changed her name to Caresse Crosby) invents a brassiere by piecing together two handkerchiefs and a ribbon. Innovative for its lack of a midsection, it is short and soft and separates the breasts naturally.

It flattens the breasts for the fashionable flapper style, popular into the mid-1920s. She receives a patent for her creation, but it is not commercially successful, partially because only those with small, firm breasts can pull it off.

1927

✿ **Cleavage Is "It"**

In the silent movie *It*, Clara Bow plays a salesclerk with her sights set on the son of a department store tycoon. After accepting an invitation to join him for dinner at the Ritz, the original "It Girl" takes a pair of scissors and cuts décolletage into her dress. This girl knew where to draw the line . . . and how to show off her assets!

Late 1920s ▶

✿ **Boom of the Bust**

Maidenform (then Maiden Form) breaks away from the flapper ideal of making breasts flatter and starts producing bras that flatter. Through the '30s, bras lift and separate, featuring new designs that enhance how women look in their outerwear. Bias-cut gowns (like the one modeled here by Claudette Colbert) in slinky fabrics require shaping underneath, and some of the most popular bras provide a very modern "uplift."

Early–mid 1930s

✿ **Measures of Success**

Finally, someone realizes that the measurement of the bust and the size of the breasts require two separate scales. Form Fit makes small, average, and full cups in each band size in 1932. Then, S. H. Camp and Company assign letters—A through D—to breast sizes (now known as cup sizes). Soon, major bra manufacturers are following this formula. During the same period, multiple fasteners and D rings appear to adjust band sizes and shoulder straps, so wearers can decide how snug to hold or how high to hoist.

1939

✿ Point Taken

The Belle Poitrine, with its circular rings of stitching that create a pointy, cone-shaped silhouette, is invented, turning breasts around the country into the pointer sisters.

1943 ▼

✿ Torpedo Tits

At the start of filming the movie *The Outlaw,* producer and airplane designer Howard

Hughes is troubled that the bras worn by the buxom Jane Russell don't properly fit her ample proportions. He designs the Cantilever bra, based on the engineering principles of bridge making, for her to wear in the movie. Women, subsequently, are on a mission to re-create the "missile" effect on their own chests. (In Martin Scorsese's 2004 movie *The Aviator,*

I dreamed I won the election in my maidenform bra

Leonardo DiCaprio, playing Hughes, notes that "the length of the actual cleavage is five inches and one-quarter.")

1949 ▲

✿ A Girl Can Dream

Maidenform launches a cutting-edge, long-running advertising campaign showing a bra-clad model taking on various "dream roles." Many ads suggest roles for women that are quite controversial for the time, such as "I dreamed I won the election . . . in my Maidenform bra."

1950s ▶

✿ Sweater Girls

This is the age of voluptuous screen stars with ample cleavage. Marilyn Monroe (top), Gina Lollobrigida, Jayne Mansfield, Sophia Loren, Elizabeth Taylor, Brigitte Bardot (middle), Anita Ekberg, Lana Turner (bottom) . . . If you're young enough not to know what these ladies have in common, here's a modern-day hint: Pamela Anderson. Less-endowed women start

boosting their busts with all forms of padding and stuffing. Unfortunately, in the throes of passion, some are embarrassed when it is discovered that tissues and socks are behind a buxom bosom, hence the advent of the term "falsies."

1960s

✿ Pill Poppers

The contraceptive pill is introduced, liberating women's sexual behavior and turning the fashion focus toward something other than just breasts. Young women start wearing more form-fitting clothing (bikinis, tight jeans) and begin to show their midriffs. Despite the downplaying of breasts, bust measurements increase almost an inch over the next two decades.

hot dates for bras

Late 1960s

☆ Bra Ban

The women's movement brings rebellion against restraint, celebrated in part by bra burnings. Nevertheless, most women continue to wear some sort of bra, however minimal, throughout the decade. Designers heed the need and start creating more comfortable, flexible styles. Most significantly, Rudi Gernreich introduces the "No Bra Bra," a soft, skintone garment that went well with unstructured styles and sheer fabrics.

1970

☆ The Emperor's New Clothes?

One of the most popular bras is the Kloss Glossie, a bra made of such sheer, stretchy, glittery material that it appears not to exist. Sheer is definitely in, a function of the free and unfettered look inspired by the women's movement as well as by advances in textile technology.

1970s

☆ Move Over, Newton

When feminists stage a protest outside Frederick's of Hollywood, its founder, Frederick Mellinger, famously responds that "the law of gravity will win out." Indeed it does, as breasts will always need

some form of support. Started in 1946, Frederick's is responsible for bringing sexy, sheer black lingerie to the white cotton underworld of America.

1977 ▼

☆ Running Mates

The fitness craze creates a demand for more seam-free, contoured shapes underneath formfitting clothing. The first sports bra is made when two women take a pair of jockstraps, cut them apart, and sew them together. They call their creation the Jogbra.

1980s ◀

☆ Undress for Success

Ooomph makes a comeback with push-up bras and demi cups. Women now operate in the corporate world and hold their

femininity close to their chests, wearing all forms of frills and lace underneath those tailored suits. Glamour returns, from luxury incarnate La Perla to Victoria's Secret's sensuously sexy silks and satins.

1990s

☆ The Wonder Years

What is often not known about the Wonderbra phenomenon is that this padded, underwire push-up bra had been introduced in Britain thirty years earlier. Relaunched in 1994 with a major media blitz, it is so popular that production can't keep up with demand. In the years that follow, a slew of competitors rise to the challenge, amplifying that famous cleavage line.

2000s

☆ The Bra-volution Continues

If I have any say in it, women will continue having bra breakthroughs as television shows, magazines, and newspapers spread the news that almost every female knows next to nothing about the single most important garment she wears.

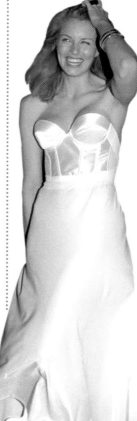

The Right Fit

When you begin your mission to find the right bra, the three most important things you need to understand are sizing, how to wear a bra properly, and how to evaluate the bras you try on.

HOW TO SIZE

There are all sorts of systems for measuring yourself. The main problem with them is . . . they don't work. These measurements are nothing more than a starting point. Just as body size, height, and weight affect overall clothing fit, busts differ in volume, shape, and spacing. Your body type goes beyond what the scale says, and your breasts are much more than a tape measure can record. And a bra that *somewhat* fits just isn't enough. You have to get it right.

The first thing to understand is that band size and cup size complement each other. They are not independent size ranges, but rather interrelated measurements. Women are always shocked when they realize this elementary point—that band and cup size are two entirely separate scales. You thought you've got your 34, 36, or 38 on one hand and you match it up with your A, your B, or your C, right? Wrong! While a 34 is always a 34, a C is *not* always a C. The numbers are absolute (they represent band width), but the cups are relative to the band size. As a band gets bigger, the "U" of the cup increases in width. So, C cups in 34, 36, and 38 are not the same. When you need to change your band size, you might also need a different cup size to compensate for the change. If you go down in band size, you might need to increase your cup size. If you go up in band size, you might need to decrease your cup size.

For example, you walk into a store and ask for a 36B. You fill out the cup, but something is still wrong—the bra rides up in the back, the wire digs into the breastbone, and the cup seems to wrinkle. My first suggestion would be to step down in band size. But if I put you into a 34 or 32, I may

Here's another shocker about bras that most women have never heard: When trying on a bra before buying, always hook the band on its loosest fitting. Why? Depending on the fabric, bras can stretch up to two inches in the back with wear and washing, and this technique will let you tighten the band as time goes on. The band should be fairly tight and firm at its biggest size. Women who assumed three hooks meant three band-size options in a single bra are surprised to discover they wear a smaller band than they believed. Many women have a lifelong habit of automatically going for the middle hook, assuming that is an indicator that the bra is the perfect size for them. Don't start out in the middle!

bump up the cup size. This means you would walk out wearing a 34C or 32D, which is not at all what you originally had in mind. While it might be the opposite case for you, the most common scenario is that women wear too big a band, and too small a cup. They leave grinning in disbelief, as if they had just lost ten pounds and got a boob job—which is precisely how the right bra can make you look. How? Well, it's not just the cups that change. As band size increases, the distance between the cups also gets wider to accommodate a larger frame. If the band is too big, your breasts hang more over the wire and are sent right and left, instead of front and

center. The relationship between band size and cup size is crucial to remember when fending for yourself in a sea of satin, spandex, lace, and elastic. If you're one of the few who knew this already, you're way ahead of the game.

MEASURE UP

The following measuring system may be what Rigby & Peller, bra fitters to the queen of England, use, but it's not how I do it. We'll get to my method afterward, but it's my duty to share the industry standard. It's important to know what the rule is so you can understand why it should be broken. If nothing else, it's interesting to see how your numbers stack up, so go ahead and try it!

There are two key measurement components: band size (such as 32, 34, 36) and cup size (the A, B, Cs). Band size is the easy part. Cup size is a more complex calculation. For accurate results, wear your best-fitting unpadded bra. A regular bra is best (nothing that minimizes or enhances your bust). It might sound strange, since we're so careful to remove every last piece of clothing before stepping on a scale, but when sizing your bust, a bra serves as a marker so you know where to measure. It's faster and easier to have someone else take

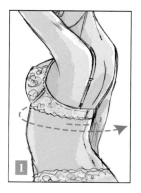

the nearest whole inch. Subtract your band size measurement from the second, larger measurement. The difference is your cup size, as listed in the chart below. For example, 36" (bust measurement) – 34" (band size) = 2" or (according to chart) a B cup.

mixed messages ◀ REBECCA'S TIP

An odd bra-sizing fact is that an AA is smaller than an A, which you'd think would mean, by extension, that a DD is smaller than a D; however, a DD is bigger than a D, and a DDD is bigger than a DD. If your eyes glaze over at all these letters, you're not the only one who's confused!

the measurements, but don't worry if you can't recruit someone for the job.

1. **Band Size** Take a measuring tape and measure the length around your rib cage directly below your bust. Make sure the measuring tape is straight and flat across your back and parallel to the floor. Pull the tape measure snugly around you. Round the measurement to the closest whole inch, either up or down. If the number is even, add four inches. If the rounded measurement is odd, add five inches. For example, 31" + 5" = 36". *Voilà!* The final number is your (supposed) band size.

2. **Cup Size** Standing, with your arms at your sides, measure around your body at the fullest part of your bust, parallel to the floor. Round this number up or down to

Difference	Standard Cup Size
0"–$^{1}/_{2}$" (1.3 cm)	AA
$^{1}/_{2}$"–1" (2.6 cm)	A
2" (5.1 cm)	B
3" (7.6 cm)	C
4" (10.2 cm)	D
5" (12.7 cm)	DD or E
6" (15.2 cm)	DDD or F
7" (17.8 cm)	G
8" (20.3 cm)	H
9" (22.9 cm)	I
10" (25.4 cm)	J

LOST IN TRANSLATION

Another confusing aspect of sizing is that each country has a different system. The table to the right is a handy converter when buying imported bras, but by no means is it absolutely accurate. Some bras, particularly those from Italy, may also come in sizes small, medium, and large or 1, 2, 3, and 4. It's best just to try on!

OFF-THE-CHART BREASTS

While we're talking about sizing, let me point out that if your breasts are on either the small or large side, you're probably used to being ignored when it comes to bras. Your size might not even be included in this chart. Most bras are made for average-size people, so what do you do if you're not "average"? Many women in these categories complain (and rightfully so) that bras don't accommodate them at all, or the choices are so few and unappealing that they feel rejected. Yes, I know it sounds a lot like dating, but these are matters we can take into our own hands.

CURVY GIRLS If you're a D cup or larger, it ain't easy finding a bra that fits, flatters, and looks fabulous. Did you know that a pair of

US	UK	France	Australia	International
32AA	32A	85A	10AA	70A
32A	32B	85B	10A	70B
32B	32C	85C	10B	70C
32C	32D	85D	10C	70D
32D	32DD	85DD	10D	70DD
34AA	34A	90A	12AA	75A
34A	34B	90B	12A	75B
34B	34C	90C	12B	75C
34C	34D	90D	12C	75D
34D	34DD	90DD	12D	75DD
34DD	34E	90E	12DD	75E
36AA	36A	95A	14AA	80A
36A	36B	95B	14A	80B
36B	36C	95C	14B	80C
36C	36D	95D	14C	80D
36D	36DD	95DD	14D	80DD
36DD	36E	95E	14DD	80E
38AA	38A	100A	16AA	85A
38A	38B	100B	16A	85B
38B	38C	100C	16B	85C
38C	38D	100D	16C	85D
38D	38DD	100DD	16D	85DD
38DD	38E	100E	16DD	85E
40A	40B	105B	18A	90B
40B	40C	105C	18B	90C
40C	40D	105D	18C	90D
40D	40DD	105DD	18D	90DD
40DD	40E	105E	18DD	90E

D-cup breasts weigh somewhere between fifteen and twenty-three pounds? The bigger the breasts, the more they move and the greater the discomfort can be. For you curvy girls, it matters that much more that your breasts get the support they need.

The first dilemma is logistical. Even in the United States, where there are supposed to be standard cup-size measurements, companies do not agree on bra-size designations once you get beyond a D cup. So what's a gal to do? First, don't get hung up on an actual number-and-letter combo. All that matters is the fit. Everyone from an A to a J cup needs to try before she buys. But to help you decipher what cup sizes bigger than a D are called, the chart on the next page breaks down the sizing codes of some major brands.

What's truly frustrating is that many designers of bigger bras assume that women with bigger chests want to downplay their breasts with a minimizing bra, when, more often than not, they want to enhance what they've got

Smooth and seamless, lacy and dainty, or a combo of both—bras for curvy girls aren't always a bust.

with something pretty. By "enhance" I don't mean that they want their breasts to appear larger, they just want to put their best breasts forward, and not have them hanging low around their waistlines or mashed under their armpits. Some minimizers work by compressing the breasts, spreading them out evenly all over the chest wall. But flattening is far from flattering. When the breasts are pressing down into the abdominal area, it can make certain types of figures look chunky, particularly short-waisted women. It's much better to lift, then divide and conquer, so your breasts appear lusciously voluptuous!

As for the bras themselves, styles designed for busty babes usually forsake fashion for function. Let's face it, most of these bras are just plain ugly. A giant, industrial-looking, flesh-colored schoolmarm bra doesn't make anyone feel very pretty. And though many companies have started making beautiful bras in bigger sizes, there are still a lot of fit issues that curvy girls have to contend with.

	Curvy Cups: Sizes D–L								
Difference between Bust & Band Measurements	4"	5"	6"	7"	8"	9"	10"	11"	12"
US Standard Cup Size	D	E	F	G	H	I	J	K	L
Aviana	D	E	F	G	H				
Bali	D	DD	DDD						
B.B. Curves	D	DD	E	F					
Chantelle	D	E	F	G					
Eprise by Lise Charmel	D	E	F						
Fantasie	D	DD	E	F	FF	G	GG		
Glamorise	D	DD	F	G	H	I			
Goddess (most styles)	D	DD	DDD	F	FF				
Gossard	D	DD	F	FF					
Lane Bryant	D	DD or E	DDD or F	FF or G	GG	H or HH	I or II		
Leading Lady	D	E	F	G	H				
Le Mystere	D	E	F	G					
Lunaire	D	DD	DDD	DDDD					
Miss Mary of Sweden		D	DD	E	F	G	G	H	
Olga	D	DD	DDD						
Panache	D	DD	E	F					
Playtex	D	DD	DDD						
Prima Donna	D	E	F						
Rigby & Peller	D	DD	E	F	FF	G	GG		
Simone Perele	D	E	F	G	H	I			
Triumph	D	E	F						
Va Bien	D	DD							
Vanity Fair	D	DD	DDD						
Wacoal	D	DD	DDD						

First off, it's often very difficult to find a style you like, or any style at all, in larger cup sizes. Determined to leave with a bra, you end up buying one with cups that are too small, thinking you can compensate by going up a band size. For example, if you are a 40E and the bra you want only goes up to a D cup, you figure you can go up a band size and down a cup size. You assume a 42D is pretty much the same, but it's not—the band is too big. If you wear a band that isn't the right size, everything is thrown off. Your breasts hang over the cups in front, the shoulder straps dig in, and the band rides up in the back. This improper fit has a lot of influence on your posture too, causing your shoulders and chest to slump over. But don't give up—there are beautiful, sexy, and more substantial bras out there.

Are you thinking, "Yeah, but how much do I have to pay for one of them?" Yes, bras can be expensive, but women with bigger cup sizes should not back away from paying higher prices. I know it sounds unfair, but usually the more you spend on a good-quality bra, the better the support. Cheap bras will cost you in the long run. Don't penny-pinch if you have large breasts! They'll be sticking around for a lot longer than a pair of designer jeans, so they're worth the investment!

BIGGIE SMALLS

Q. **My breasts are two different sizes—what should I do?**

A. Never fear! Many twins are not identical. Look for contour bras that mold your breasts and maintain a uniform shape. If the discrepancy is too great, wear a fiber-filled push-up bra into which a removable pad, known as a cookie, can be added on the smaller side. Another solution is a silicone insert—it looks and feels real and can be placed on the smaller side for perfect balance. If someone brushes up against you, he'll never know.

SMALL WONDERS The well-endowed aren't the only ones ignored by most bra companies. If your breasts are in the A or small B range (or maybe you thought you were more like an undershirt size, on a good day), you've probably noticed that the selection in your size is equally limited. While the obvious padded styles frequently come in an A or AA, the really lovely, more unusual styles often start at a B. That's just a general rule, and there are many styles that will fit—and

A slinky cami does a lot for girls on the A-list.

A WORD FOR THE "LITTLE LADIES"

I know that many smaller-breasted women often wear undershirts or camisoles instead of bras, but these do nothing to enhance your natural assets. Even an A cup has needs:

Definition: A contour bra with or without light padding will create a natural-looking shape and hint at some cleavage.

Support: It doesn't matter that you're not aspiring for a bodacious bosom—your tissue and muscles need support. Okay, I confess that I spent a lot of my younger days braless. Not a good idea! Even A breasts that are firm at, say, fifteen years of age will in time become jiggly and wiggly.

even more reasons to be happy with what you've got. While there is something to that lusty, heaving bosom look, small-breasted women have the freedom to choose the times when they want the boobage (with padding) and the times they don't. Plenty of women would kill to be able to wear a camisole without extra support or even to wear one without feeling like there are two giant magnets on her chest attracting every set of male eyes. You, and only you, are the ones who can wear the flimsy little nothings that send the big-breasted running for backup. Also,

while big breasts might look tantalizing hidden underneath clothing, bountiful busts are a lot to be reckoned with. And because breasts naturally head downhill as you get older, smaller breasts fare better in the test of time. While all shapes and sizes are subject to stretch marks, the pull of gravity takes its toll more dramatically on larger breasts. Your blessed chest is low-maintenance; upkeep on big breasts is a lot more challenging. If all these reasons aren't enough to make you grateful for what you've got, you can always fake it with foam padding or silicone inserts.

MY METHOD

*S*o, I promised you earlier that I would tell you my nonmeasuring system for figuring out what size you are. I hope you haven't been holding your breath. Let me start by saying that I never touch a tape measure myself (and certainly don't bother with the math), but I realize that leaves you hanging, so to speak. **The truth is,** my method all comes down to trial and error. By understanding how sizing works (which you now know) and how a bra should and should not fit (which you'll soon know), you'll be able to tell what's right for you. Trust me, this knowledge is much more useful than any system of measurement.

STUCK IN THE MIDDLE

Q. **What if I'm between sizes?**

A. What if you're a 33? Cheer up—an odd number doesn't mean you're an oddball. When trying on bras, try both size 32s and 34s. Depending on the brand, one will fit better than the other. If that doesn't work, buy the bigger size and take the bra to a seamstress who can take in the band for you—an easy and inexpensive task. Some better lingerie stores offer in-house alterations. We alter our clothes, why not our bras?

WEIGHT TRAINING

Q. **My weight changes a lot, and there are times of the month when my bras are too tight or too loose. What do I do?**

A. If your weight frequently fluctuates, diversify your bra collection so you can accommodate your breasts when a slightly different bra size is in order. Keep in mind that some bras are made of stiffer fabrics, while others are more elastic and stretchy. Front-closure bras have less flexibility

when it comes to adjusting for slight weight gain or bloating. With a back closure, you have the option to adjust to three positions.

BIG BAND WIDTH

Q. **I'm a D cup, and all the bras in my size have bands that are wide in the sides and the back. Why can't I find more delicate, skinny bands that fit?**

A. It's understandable that you long to wear the dainty, narrow bands of smaller bras, but they aren't practical for bigger breasts. In fact, skinnier bands will look worse. Skinny-size bands will cinch you in, creating a sausagelike effect of creases and rolls. The wider bands and straps provide the necessary support, which will encourage you to stand tall and proud while your breasts stand up and out. Wider bands are also less likely to ride up in the back. Do you remember that the average D cup breasts weigh about fifteen to twenty-three pounds? Imagine tiny spaghettilike straps digging into your shoulders trying to hold up that weight. It would

feel like a metal wire against your skin. There is a legitimate reason for larger sizes not being made any other way. It's physics, after all.

FOR THE BROADS

Q. **My back is very broad, but my breasts are on the smaller side. If the band fits, the cups are always too big. Do I have to choose between the right band size and the right cup size? Can't a girl have it all?**

A. A bra is greater than the sum of its parts, so it's hard to break down the components when the overall fit matters most. I recommend finding the best bra fit you can, favoring a proper cup size over a band that is slightly too small across your back. The reason I suggest this is because bra extenders—simple little attachments with hooks—are an easy solution that allows you to adjust the band size to fit the width of your rib cage. If you are a difficult fit, come to the dressing room armed with bra extenders, so you can play around till you get it right.

HOW TO WEAR A BRA

Wearing a bra properly is all about product placement. Follow these steps every time you *wear* a bra, not just when you're trying one on.

1. Stand in front of a mirror. Slip your arms through the bra's shoulder straps.

2. Bring the bra up so that the band is just under your breasts.

3. As you clasp the band in the back, lean forward slightly to place your breasts into each cup.

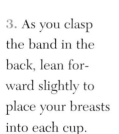

4. Clasp the bra on the loosest hook first. See if it is comfortable in this position. If it needs to be tighter, go to the second hook, and so on.

5. Stand up and adjust the shoulder straps over your shoulders.

6. Adjust the straps so they share the task of holding up your breasts.

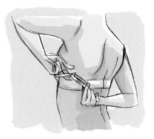

7. While looking at yourself in the mirror, move your breasts around with your hand until they are fully in the cup.

Your nipples should be front and center, facing forward like headlights. The cup should contain the entire breast, unless you are wearing a demi or push-up style. There should be no spillage. Note that adjusting with your hands requires looking in the mirror—no putting the bra on blind.

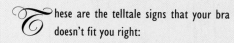 hooked

There are other ways to position your breasts when you wear a bra. Here are two common methods.

Bend-&-Shake: A DO! **Slip your arms into the bra, bend at the waist (just like in step 3, left). Shake your breasts so they fall into place, letting the full volume fill the cups, before reaching back and fastening yourself in. Then, follow the rest of the steps to refine your bustline. This method applies more to someone who has a lot of breast tissue, especially a D or more. An A or B cup lady has little need for bending over to place her breasts, but everyone should check for centering!**

Hook-&-Twist: A DON'T! **A lot of women opt to hook the bra in front around their waist, then twist it around and pull it up, like they saw their grannies do it. Unless you are physically limited and unable to get your arms behind your back, do not use this method. You could end up hooking the bra at a random place so the band doesn't fit properly, wear down the inner elastic in the twisting motion, and miss out on the beneficial stretch of reaching your arms back behind you.**

low riders or high flyers?

Make sure your bra lifts your breasts to the right height by taking this little test: Measure the distance from the top of your shoulder to the crook in your elbow. Find the midpoint. Your nipples should be parallel to this point, halfway between shoulder and elbow. If they are not, try shortening the straps a bit for that extra lift.

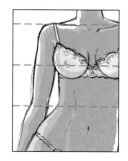

BAD BRA!

*T*hese are the telltale signs that your bra doesn't fit you right:

* Red, painful shoulders

* Indents or grooves on your shoulder or body after prolonged wear

* Frequent need for shoulder strap adjustment and repositioning

* Uncomfortable or excessive perspiration in your cleavage, especially in warm weather

* A lumpy and bumpy look under tops

* Numbness in arms or fingers caused by reduced circulation (Note: These are two symptoms that can be very serious. If this is something you have experienced, investigate the fit of your bra to see if it plays a role—and see a doctor.)

HOOKING UP

Q. How many sets of vertical hooks should be on my bra closure?

A. The sets of hooks are based on the width of the band at the back closure, which, in turn, is proportionate to cup size. Small cup sizes only need one or two sets of vertical hooks to hold the band in place. For bigger cup sizes, the more the merrier. For proper support, bands will have anywhere from three to five or more hooks.

THE THREE FACTORS OF FIT

Now that you're wearing your bra correctly and understand how sizing works, it's time to judge the fit. You'll need to consider **1) the band, 2) the straps, and 3) the cups.**

BANDS. You're sure you wear a 34 bra. You've always worn a 34 bra. Well, does that 34 bra make a perfect circle under your rib cage? Is the band snug, but not so tight you can't fit a finger underneath? If not, your band is the wrong size.

The next step is figuring out if your band is too small or too loose. The majority of women wear bras with bands that are too big, but if you're in the minority whose bra is uncomfortable or tight—yes, it's true, you're not supposed to suffer—or if the band creates rolls of flesh above and below the side wings, your band is too small.

Nine times out of ten, a woman wearing the wrong size bra is guilty of overexaggerating her band size. The telltale signs: A band that rides up in the back. Breast tissue peeking out underneath the bra. Clasps that come undone. Straps that constantly fall off your shoulders. Even that old demon—back flab. I know, I know. I just said that a band that was too loose creates back fat. Well, so can one that's too loose, because if the band moves around, you end up looking fleshy.

back fat

Don't blame your body for this one. Many women mistakenly think that the flesh that bulges up around the band and under the armpits would go away if they lost some weight. Maybe. But did you ever notice the muffin-top effect of too-tight low-rise jeans? Same goes for back flab. It's caused by a bra band that creeps up, pushing soft tissue up with it. The good news is that the pouch can be reduced by wearing a band that is snug, level across the back, and sitting below the shoulder blades.

Of course, any strip of elastic that holds skin in will create some sort of indent. But remember, you are a woman, and nature designed you to have a pleasing layer of flesh over your frame. Everyone has it, it's perfectly normal, and nobody is looking at your back as closely as you are. Besides, if your bra is working, they won't be looking at your back at all.

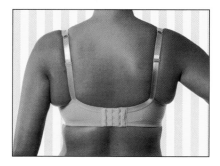

THE BAND THAT'S TOO SMALL

If you're seeing rolls of flesh around the side wings, it's likely that the band is too tight, cinching the skin.

STRAPS. Unlike bands and cups, which have to do with size, straps are often a matter of the bra style. Though many women don't bother, straps should be adjusted—daily—particularly as the bra ages and begins to loosen up. What you're aiming for is a bra that is absolutely level across the back. But you don't want to achieve that look by overtightening your straps to the point that they dig into your shoulders. (That usually means your band is too loose.) In no case should the main support for your bra fall on the straps alone. That's the band's job; the straps should be just tight enough to hold the bra in place on your shoulders. Anything tighter than that will lead to a bra that rides up, and the much more serious possibility of neck, back, and shoulder pain. So remember: Straps should share the weight, not bear the weight.

the strap-to-band ratio test

◀ **REBECCA'S TIP**

To tell if your straps are adjusted correctly and not bearing too much of the burden, slip the straps off your shoulders so they rest on your arms. Your bra should stay up and remain in place without the help of the straps. It's okay if the cups flop over, but the band should not budge.

  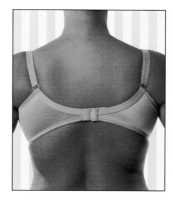

THE BAND THAT'S TOO BIG

1. Breast spillage is proof that either your band is too big or your cups are too small.

2. If you're always pushing and pulling at the band, you need to go down in band size.

3. Since narrow shoulders usually equal narrow rib cage, a too-large band will ride up. Some women compensate by tightening the straps to the shortest length. Ouch.

REBECCA'S TIP ▶ strap struggles

Do your bra straps pinch your shoulders? This doesn't necessarily mean they're too tight. You might need a bra that is more supportive or has thicker shoulder straps.

Are your straps constantly falling off your shoulders? The unsuspected culprit might actually be too big a band. If the band is fine, and tightening doesn't work, try a different style. Demi bras, for example, tend to have wider-set straps than other bras. If you have very sloped shoulders, try a racerback front-closure style. Another option is professional tailoring. Bra straps can always be altered—a simple task in the hands of a seamstress. Like jeans, straps often run a little long, offering flexibility in case they need a nip and tuck.

GETTING THE STRAP

Q. I have big breasts and find that straps always dig into my shoulders, even on bras with wider straps. Is it because my breasts are so heavy?

A. Often straps dig into shoulders when the support isn't properly distributed. If your band doesn't give enough support, the shoulder straps have to, literally, pick up the weight. No matter the width, bra straps are not cut out for this role—they are supposed to be costars, not the principle actors of this show. Painful straps are part of an overall problem with fit, not a problem with your breasts. You need only look for another size or style. You can also purchase specially designed strap cushions (available at notions stores), which will ease the pain and pressure on overburdened, sensitive shoulders.

CUPS. I know it's a lot to keep in mind, but now that you know about bands and straps, it's time to turn to the alphabet soup of cups. So, let's start with cups that are too big. To begin with, cups should never, ever pucker up. (That's doubly bad: No support, and wrinkles that show through your clothing.) Unless you're wearing a demi-cup bra, your breasts should fill both the top and bottom portion of the bra.

THE CUPS ARE TOO BIG

A wrinkly bra, with extra looseness at the top, means you should try a smaller cup, or even a different bra style—perhaps a demi cup.

But what if your issue is less about wrinkles and more about overflow? Chances are you should go up a cup size. Other warning signs: squished breasts and underwire that doesn't lie flat or pokes the breast tissue.

 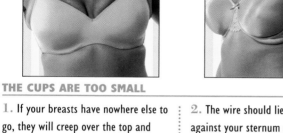 

THE CUPS ARE TOO SMALL

1. If your breasts have nowhere else to go, they will creep over the top and spill out the sides of the bra. If the cup runneth over, go up a size.

2. The wire should lie smoothly against your sternum and ribs. There may be a space if your sternum is deep-set, and that's fine. But if the wire ever rests on top of the breast tissue itself, go up a cup.

3. An underwire should arc around the breasts, not poke into them. If it does, you need a larger cup with enough width to hold your entire breast.

 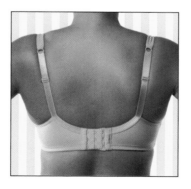 

THE PERFECT FITTING BRA

1. Snug, but you can still fit a finger underneath.

2. A firm fit around your back, since that's where most of the support comes from.

3. The front and back of the band should be even and parallel to the ground.

Bra Shopping

When most women look for a bra, they have style rather than size in mind, but I had to make sure you ate your dinner before your dessert. Now that we've got sizing and fit down, though, we can get to the fun part . . . shopping.

So, let's start with the age-old question I always hear when women talk about bra shopping: *Why buy a bra for fifty dollars when I can buy two for the same price?* There are so many styles out there that are pretty, practical, and inexpensive, why spend more? The easy answer is that when it comes to bras, you get what you pay for. Many women have wondered why something so small that uses so little fabric should cost so much. While fabric quality plays a part, the fabric is not the major cost. It's the labor. The bra is one of the most complex pieces of lingerie ever created. It is a matter not simply of looks, but also of engineering: Some bras are composed of up to almost fifty compo-

nents. These pretty little nothings are designed with a structure and function comparable to a suspension bridge. We're talking architecture for the feminine body. A more expensive price tag on a bra usually implies better craftsmanship, which translates into better comfort and fit. **It is worth the extra money to buy bras that you actually feel comfortable wearing, particularly if you are a C cup or more;** otherwise, you'll spend your life in varying degrees of bra discomfort, always adjusting and futzing with something. Or worse, you'll buy bras that you'll never wear. Trust me, fifty bucks is nothing compared to all the times you have to tug at your annoying bra.

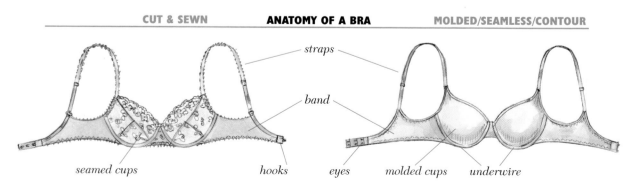

CUT & SEWN　　**ANATOMY OF A BRA**　　MOLDED/SEAMLESS/CONTOUR

straps

band

seamed cups　　*hooks*　　*eyes*　　*molded cups*　　*underwire*

Still, even a lingerie diva such as myself knows that not everybody can shell out a small fortune for a bra. Fine, don't spend a ton. You don't have to. Just remember what you now know about bra fit and don't walk out of any store—mass-market or boutique—unless you, and only you, are comfortable with how that bra feels and looks. It's a cliché, but it's true: An educated consumer is a smart consumer. And a smart consumer doesn't settle. A bra doesn't have to be outrageously expensive, but it's not worth a nickel if it doesn't fit you properly.

In addition to the comfort, there is the fabric factor. Here we're talking quality, not quantity. The design and details of more expensive bras are really visible if you look more closely. But, again, whatever your price range, you deserve a bra with nicely

BARE TRUTH

Cleavage refers to the line or cleft between a woman's breasts (not the fullness above the breasts created by a push-up). It comes from the word *cleave*, which means to split or divide in two.

Décolletage is a noun that refers to the plunging front neckline of a woman's low-cut garment (or to the garment itself). A woman's body does not have décolletage, but rather *décolleté,* a noun that refers to the upper part of a woman's chest. Décolleté is also an adjective used to describe a garment that has a low-cut neckline.

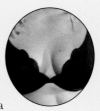

REBECCA'S TIP ▶ shopping tip short list

When setting out to go bra shopping, be prepared to spend some time on your quest. You'll probably need to try on several styles. Be willing to experiment with sizes. If something looks or feels askew, don't abandon the style before trying a different band size and adjusting the cup size accordingly. As long as there are fitting rooms, it's absolutely mandatory to try, try, and try things on again. Even if you're skeptical about the salesperson's judgment, shy about baring your breasts, or feel like a pest, try to get a second opinion if you can. Believe me, nobody working in a lingerie section will be fazed.

finished seams and trims, and carefully sewn-on elastic. Better craftsmanship means better quality, which means a more durable bra that won't fall apart.

And then, let's not forget the incredible feeling that comes from wearing a fabulous bra. There's something so gratifying about indulging yourself in this private little pleasure. Buy bras that make you feel pretty. You'll feel amazing every time you put them on. Now go shop 'til your boobs don't drop!

bra-ssary

*W*hen it comes time to plan your bra wardrobe, consider the 3 Cs:

❀ Cut (plunge styles for low-cut tops, strapless bras for spaghetti straps, and so on)

❀ Content (seamless styles for sheer or clingy fabric)

❀ Color (nude to wear under white or light colors; dark for darks)

Balconet/Balconnette

Pronounced bal-kuh-nay, it has wide-set straps and less coverage than a demi bra. The effect is uplift and fullness above the breasts, as if they were being served up on a tray or standing high on a balcony.

Bralet or Bralette

An unlined wireless bra that either pulls over the head or clasps in back. Lacking significant support features such as underwires, which offer form and additional support, this style is best for smaller bustlines, a more relaxed look, or for sleepwear.

Bust Enhancers

Anything that gives the illusion of a fuller bosom. These days enhancers can be built into bras themselves, creating a far better look than the falsies of yesteryear. The Wonderbra was just the beginning!

Comfort Straps

Softly padded, lined, or wider than normal straps that increase comfort—essential for any fuller busted woman who has experienced shoulder and neck pain from the weight of her breasts pulling her bra straps down into her shoulders. Bras shouldn't be a pain in the neck!

Contour

A molded or cut-and-sewn bra designed with a fiberfill or foam lining to provide definition and shape. Because of the lining, nipple show-through is eliminated. Contour cups don't increase size; instead, they create a rounder, more symmetrical bustline.

Convertible (backless and halter)

A bra designed with modifiable and sometimes detachable straps to be worn under halter, racerback, cross-back, one-shoulder, or low-back garments. The halter feature, with straps that go behind the neck, leaves shoulders and upper back bare.

Despite being "backless," this style often is low-back rather than no-back, with closures at waist level. For a completely backless look, try a self-adhesive bra.

Bust Minimizer

A bra that gives the appearance of a reduced cup size by either mashing down the bustline or lifting and redistributing breast tissue to give the appearance of a trimmer figure. A style that does the latter is more flattering.

Bustier/Corset

An often strapless, fitted one-piece bodice that extends from bust to waist or hip, worn to support and sustain a given shape. Usually stiffened with flexible metal or plastic boning and closed in the front or back with hooks and eyes or lacing.

DAILY DEMI DILEMMA

Q. **Are demi bras considered everyday bras, or are they more appropriate for special occasions?**

A. Because the cups of demi bras cover less of the breasts, many believe this very sexy style is more of a big-night-out kind of thing. Don't punish your demi bra for being so fabulous! If it's comfortable enough for everyday, wear it—today, tonight, whenever. Note: Demi bras are not for every figure. They generally look better on breasts that are firmer or wider set. A proper fit prevents flattening of the breasts or overflowing of the cups, which can produce unsightly ripples and the double-bubble of the quad-boob look.

Demi Cup

A popular underwire with cups that are partially cut away to expose the top part of the breast (*demi* means "half"). With less coverage than a full cup, and more than a balconet, it's sexy and flattering, and perfect for low-cut, squared necklines.

Front Closure Bra

As the name implies, a bra that fastens in the front. This style makes it easier to put your bra on and take it off. On the downside, the band does not allow for the adjustments of a back-closure bra, which usually has at least three settings. (It may also confuse guys.)

Full Cup/Full Coverage

A bra that covers most of the breast, offering more coverage and support than a demi-cup bra. A full cup fits a fuller figure well and is perfect under a T-shirt.

contour misconceptions ◀ **TIP**

Did you know that contour bras do not make you look bigger? Many women buy them thinking the thin foam lining will make their breasts appear fuller—which is also why women with larger breasts shy away from them. Both groups are wrong. Contour bras make you look better, providing extra support and beautiful shaping. If you're looking for bigger, go with a padded bra.

bra-ssary

Full-Figure Bra

The term often used to designate a bra specifically designed for a more voluptuous woman. Cups tend to run larger in size than regular bras.

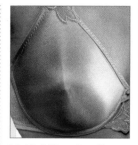

Molded/Seamless Bra

Because of a process in which a flat piece of fabric is heat-molded to form the cup shape, this one is ideal to wear underneath T-shirts and other smooth or tight-fitting tops. The only problem? Most seamless unlined bras made of stretch material don't offer the best support to larger busts.

Padded Bra

Any bra that contains padding in the cups to add fullness. Graduated padding, thicker at the base of the cups, provides a natural, enhanced look. These bras sometimes come with crescent-shaped, removable demi pads ("cookies") to give some extra oomph.

Plunge Bra

A bra with a very low, plunging front, angled cups, and thin center gore, this style is good for deep V-necklines. It is sometimes lined or padded to create center cleavage. How low will you go?

 REBECCA'S TIP divided issue

The valley can't exist without the hills. And having cleavage requires a certain amount of material to work with. You simply can't have natural cleavage with an A cup—you need at least a B. But big breasts don't guarantee cleft. It depends on the position of your breasts on your chest, since cleavage demands that your breasts be pushed together. Even plastic surgery cannot create cleavage. The good news is, cleavage can be a happy side effect of, you guessed it, wearing the right bra: a demi cup plunge bra that has crescent-shaped padding inside the cup or on the side to push the breasts into the center for the desired décolleté.

Seamed/Cut-and-Sewn

A bra with cups constructed out of carefully cut pieces of fabric that are then sewn together to form the rounded shape of a breast. The cups consist of two or more sections; generally, the more seams, the more support.

Soft Cup/No-Wire Bra

Available in many shapes and styles, a bra without wire that provides light support. Best for the smaller and firmer busted, or for when you just want a break from wearing an underwire bra.

Push-Up Bra

Designed to give the appearance of a fuller bust, an underwire bra emphasizes the breasts by lifting them high. Padding or angled cups can create center cleavage.

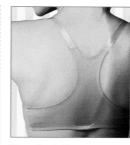

Racerback Bra

A must-have bra for summer, worn under sleeveless tops and tanks, it features back straps that curve away from the shoulder blades. Many front-close styles are racerback and most convertible bras can be adjusted that way. Particularly good for women with narrow or sloped shoulders.

Sports Bra

Sports bras protect chest ligaments and prevent breast tissue damage. Compression styles are best for smaller cup sizes, while more structured harness styles, which encapsulate each breast, are best for women who wear larger cups.

Strapless/Bandeau Bra

These bras come without shoulder straps and are usually lined with silicone or rubber strips on the inner edges to help keep the bra from slipping down. They can be underwire, seamless, push-up, padded—or bandeau, which is more like a rectangular tube.

HALFWAY . . . OR ALL THE WAY?

Q. **What's the difference between a push-up and a demi bra?**

A. The word *demi* means half or small; hence, a demi bra is more like a half-cup bra. A push-up bra is strategically designed to do just that—push up the breasts for an exaggerated lift. Some styles come with permanent or removable pads to enhance or create more cleavage. To my mind, push-ups are the bra equivalent of stiletto heels: They look hot but are usually for special occasions. Still, if every day is a special occasion in your book, then go for it!

WIRE OR NOT

Q. **How do I know whether I need an underwire?**

A. No one *needs* an underwire, but if you're a C cup or larger, you may want the added support. Soft-cup bras might seem ideal, but the temporary comfort is like sleeping on a super-soft bed—it feels fabulous but can be bad for your back. Plus, larger breasts in nonwire bras usually slant downward and have that uni-boob look. If underwires are stabbing or jabbing, look for a bra with extra padding in the wire casing.

Technological advances have led to nonwire models that give support through strategically placed elastic reinforcements and seams. The key is to make sure you are properly supported. And, of course, I want you to look good. An underwire's ability to lift, separate, and define is unparalleled. A B-cup gal looks better wearing an underwire, and an A-cupper sometimes wants to enhance what she's got.

WHAT TO WEAR UNDER THERE

Outside: Tank, halter, or strapless top

Inside: Convertible bra

When regular bra straps will show, try a strapless bustier or a convertible bra. Convertible bras can often be worn up to three ways to support almost every type of top. To be realistic, though, convertible styles do not often go over a C or D cup.

WHAT TO WEAR UNDER THERE

Outside: Deep V-neckline

Inside: Plunge bra

If you don't want any bra peek-a-boo, you might opt for a deeply plunging bra. (Don't be afraid to let a little tease of lace pop out the top.) Another option is a stick-on adhesive bra especially made for this purpose.

WHAT TO WEAR UNDER THERE

Outside: Bulky sweater

Inside: Shapely bra

Wear any bra you like, as long as it provides shaping. You don't want to look like a shapeless sack of potatoes even in a nice big sweater. There's a difference between frumpy and comfy!

wrong

right

WHAT TO WEAR UNDER THERE

Outside: T-shirts and fitted sweaters

Inside: Seamless, full-coverage bra

If you're wearing a smooth fitted top, a seamless, full-coverage bra is the way to go; otherwise, you'll be turning your chest area into a topographical map. While demi bras are flattering for breasts, they can be less kind under T-shirts—if the top of the cup divides the breast, it can create the dreaded four-boob look. If the demi fits properly, you shouldn't have to fight the battle of the bulges, but make sure to check yourself before you wreck yourself.

wrong

right

WHAT TO WEAR UNDER THERE

Outside: Racerback top

Inside: Racerback bra

How many times do you have to tuck your bra straps under your racerback tank? When you don't want your bra straps showing under your favorite muscle T, the front-closure racerback style is the solution.

WHAT TO WEAR UNDER THERE

Outside: Sheer or white top

Inside: Flesh-colored bra or camisole

Wear a flesh-colored seamless bra or camisole underneath for a subtle, more opaque look, or a bright-colored or patterned camisole for something more dramatic.

Nowadays, many brands carry a wide range of colors that blend with all different skin tones. Don't worry if the color isn't an exact match—a close approximation will do the disappearing trick.

WHAT TO WEAR UNDER THERE

Outside: Strapless

Inside: Strapless bra

Since strapless bras must be worn a little tighter in the band than regular two-strap bras, some women save the potential discomfort for the irregular formal occasion. (The heavier the breasts, the tighter the bra needs to be.)

WHAT TO WEAR UNDER THERE

Outside: Spaghetti straps

Inside: Matching or contrasting straps

I hate to be picky, but bra straps, faded or pilled from numerous washings, undermine the delicate look of spaghetti-strap tank tops. If you don't want to wear a strapless bra, find one with matching or pleasantly contrasting straps that work with the garment, or a bra with clear straps.

WHAT TO WEAR UNDER THERE . . . ADHESIVES

Outside: Deeeeeeep plunge

Inside: Reveal adhesive bra

If you're wearing a deeply plunging neckline (think of Jennifer Lopez's infamous, barely-there green dress) where regular elliptical-, crescent-, or semicircle-shaped cups stick out too much in the middle, there is finally a support solution. Called a Reveal adhesive bra, it consists of two triangles made of featherlight, super sticking flesh toned surgical tape. This style works against gravity, since you can stick the narrow top of the triangles wherever you want for more or less hoist. Mind you, beyond a D cup you may need to wear several on each breast, but I've seen it done successfully.

Outside: Backless or strapless (with no boost needed underneath)

Inside: Disposable adhesive bra

If you don't require any extra oomph under one of those numbers that basically makes it impossible to wear any regular bra, stick with a disposable stick-on one. These thin adhesive sheets simply adhere to your breasts; they support and lift, without padding. Stick-ons are sold by cup size, but if you're in doubt, go up a size so there is enough sticky surface to go around—you can always trim the excess to make sure no edges peek out. A favorite for decades, this is the real miracle bra.

Outside: Strapless and backless (and you need a boost underneath)

Inside: Reusable adhesive bra

Try a reusable adhesive bra constructed of silicone. Though it's shaped like a chicken cutlet, this ultra-effective option creates a natural look with a bit more fullness. Just position the cups on your breasts, adjusting them to get the cleavage you want, then clip the cups together in the middle and you're good to go. The adhesive sticks to your body, so you don't have to keep readjusting—as long as you follow the step-by-step directions that come with the bra. Trust me on this one: I'm someone who regularly tosses directions to the wind and learned that lesson the hard way! Also, be sure your skin is dry and free of any lotion, powder, or perfume when you apply the bra.

Outside: Spaghetti strap or strapless tops (and you don't need a bra)

Inside: Nippets

Even if support isn't an issue, no girl in a sheer or clingy top wants to feel self-conscious when a cold wind blows. Let's face it, the old Band-Aid trick has had its day; now when you want to go braless, adhesive nipple covers like Petal Tops are the perfect solution to this dilemma.

For when it's a tad nippy . . .

what to wear under there

Outside: Wedding dress

Inside: Bustier

Many wedding dresses are designed to accommodate a bustier or corset underneath. Go for it—you'll feel great. Wearing a corset enhances your figure, making you feel—and look—taller; it forces you to stand erect and pushes up your breasts. But you want to be comfortable, too. So if you're spilling out of the top or side of the cups, go up a cup size or try a different style. Whatever style you choose, if the fabric of your dress is lightweight or clingy, look for undergarments that are absolutely smooth. If the fabric has some weight and texture, you can get something more ornate or embellished, since it won't show through.

Here's a tip: Take the underwear you plan to wear on your wedding day to your bridal gown fitting.

Colors and Fabrics

When people think about underwear, they tend to think white. And that's the color they immediately turn to on an underwear shopping spree. But the real staple should be skin-colored—the right color to wear under clothing that is white, light colored, crocheted, or lacy (it blends in with your skin for a more finished look). Personally, I love colors and can't resist wearing contrasting bras with my tops and dresses—what can I say, I'm a colorful person!

When I started my business in the late 1970s, lingerie was much more feminine. Bra fabrics were luxurious—all pure silk and lace. While these lovely little numbers still exist, there are a lot more basic and synthetic designs out now. Most women just want an absolutely smooth appearance under their clothing, which is nice and practical, but also boring. Don't get me wrong, the clean look of a perfect seamless bra under a T-shirt is unparalleled, but it's like eating the same old cereal every day for breakfast. Sometimes you want the eggs Benedict. So, here's to knowing you don't always have to be predictable, always thinking about what's practical and forgetting what's pretty. I love the more sensuous bras—not just plain old

Have a little fun with color and texture.

microfiber and stretch satins, but bras made with silks, eyelets, laces, and velvets—the ones that make you feel gorgeous and that make guys go crazy. Why not wear a vibrantly colored balconet for that serve-it-up-on-a-platter, "take me now!" look? Maybe not for every day, but at least every once in a while. I wear mine for no particular reason at all, with my jeans and camisoles. I like to pamper myself 24/7, not just save special things for special occasions.

Whether you buy bras to celebrate your breasts or to try to hide them, there are certain essentials you should possess in your collection. For everyday wear, you should have at least a week's worth of bras in your daily rotation. It's also good to have different bras for seasonal changes. Lightweight cotton bras are cooler and more comfortable when it's hot, hot, hot (and for once I'm not talking about the bedroom). These everyday bras are your staples—the supportive ones you can count on. If you find a style you love, my advice is to buy more than one. The perfect bra doesn't come along every day, and it will last a lot longer if you don't wear it daily.

KEEPING YOUR COOL

Q. **I have pretty big breasts and my cleavage gets really sweaty, especially in warm weather. Is there anything I can do to stop feeling like I have the Panama Canal running down my chest?**

A. Let's face it, we start to sweat anywhere our body has creases and can't breathe—our bottoms, our armpits, and, for those with bigger chests, in our cleavage and under our breasts. If your bra squeezes your breasts too close, try a style that provides more separation. Some materials are notoriously less breathable than others, so keep fabric content in mind when shopping. Another option is a full-coverage bra with lacy perforated cutouts that allow air to circulate. The ventilation lets skin breathe and helps keep you cool.

YOU SAY GOOD-BYE, WE SAY HELLO

Q. **My favorite bra has been discontinued. I feel like I've been dumped. Will I ever find another that fits so well?**

A. All is not lost! In this situation, the right match just might be another member of your ex's family. If you have a tried-and-true bra that is now discontinued, try on similar products from the manufacturer you know and love. Makers usually create bras that are consistent with their signature style shape, and very often they update your old favorite into newer collections. You might be pleasantly surprised by the family resemblance. When all else fails, it may be time to look for a new bra look and style altogether.

THE REPLACEMENTS

Q. **How often should I replace my bra?**

A. The answer depends on several variables, including how much and how often your body changes, how frequently you wear a particular bra, and how you care for it (and we'll get to this in "Long Live Lingerie: Care and Upkeep" on page 165). Generally, you should replace your bra anywhere from every six months to every two years. I know, our bras begin to feel like old friends and they can be hard to part with, but once they stop doing what they were intended to do, it's time to say good-bye. No coquette should be caught wearing a stretched-out bra with those little squiggles of elastic popping through. Out with the old, in with the new!

Special Bras

GOOD SPORTS
Athletic Bras

While a regular bra is designed to provide support, a sports bra is designed for mega-support. It keeps the breasts from moving around during strenuous activities. **Even if your pecs are perfectly toned, breasts are not made of muscle, so no amount of exercise can tone the actual breast tissue.** If the ligaments that attach the breasts to the chest aren't supported, gravity and motion will eventually wear them down and breast support and positioning will deteriorate. In addition to the long-term sag effects, who wants to get their lovely lacy bras all sweaty and soiled while climbing the StairMaster anyway?

I'm the biggest advocate of wearing a beautiful bra at all times, but when you're hitting the gym, wearing anything but a sports bra would be like wearing stilettos on a treadmill. Not too smart, and dangerous.

Sport support has long-term impact.

Women with smaller breasts are better off with compression-style sports bras that flatten the breasts, preventing jiggling by keeping them near and dear. Women with larger breasts should go for bras with separate molded cups that encapsulate each breast—not the flattened uni-boob shape of the pull-over, no-cup styles. Divide and conquer is the best tactic. How much support you need depends on the impact level of your activity and the size of your breasts. Basically, you want to minimize bounce as much as possible.

When shopping, one of the main things to be aware of is the fabric. Bras that are mostly cotton get heavy with perspiration, so look for fabrics that have moisture-wicking properties. Zippers or clasps should always have padding between you and the garment to avoid irritation. Inner seams should be flat and soft. And don't think you can get away without trying on a sports bra before buying it.

In the dressing room, jump up and down and swing your arms to check for comfort and support. If the elastic under the bustline moves, the shoulder straps slip, or your breasts bulge out of the sides near the armpits, the bra doesn't fit.

Today, most sports bras have snaps or some other form of closure so you can get in and out of it easily and receive better support for a flattering, instead of flattening, effect. You never know who you might run in to! I recommend replacing sports bras every six to twelve months, and sometimes more often, depending on your activity level. I know that's hard to do, especially because sports bras aren't the most exciting purchase for most of us, but as soon as a bra starts to loosen up, it's time to toss it.

MATERNAL FIGURES
Bras

Let me state the obvious: Your breasts change during and after pregnancy . . . a lot. The process of getting to temporary milkmaid status, with the prerequisite ample bosom, comes with its own growing pains. Wearing the right bra can alleviate one of the discomforts of pregnancy while letting you enjoy your newfound ample bosom.

MATERNITY While every pregnancy is different, most women find they need a new bra several times during the nine months of pregnancy. As breasts enlarge and get heavier, new sensitivities develop to certain fabrics and anything that binds. Breasts become tender, at which time some women like more, and others like less, support. It all depends on how much your breasts change during your pregnancy, which is as unique a process as the changes going on in the rest of your body.

Women usually need to make the switch to a larger bra at around the third to fourth month of pregnancy, when their breasts start to swell. When shopping for a maternity bra, it's better to make an investment in a quality one that can accommodate your body as it changes.

A properly fitted underwire bra should be fine, though a soft cup is often more comfortable for those who are sensitive to the wire, especially when the breasts are at their fullest. If you do wear a wire, it is imperative that the bra fit correctly, because pressure on the milk ducts under the arms can cause medical complications.

Either way, find a bra with wider side bands and shoulder straps for added support. The straps should have some cushioning and should not stretch. The band needs to have at least three back-closure settings for flexibility in fit.

A word of caution: Your band size will change as your ribs move to make room for the baby, so you need to be able to lengthen it. Contrary to my advice for fitting a regular bra (which should be tried on at its loosest setting), **a maternity bra should at first fit at its tightest setting,** which lets you adjust to the loosest hook when you're about to pop. If you find your bra is too tight in circumference, try a bra extender (see page 41) or toss your first maternity bra and get a bigger one.

NURSING When the time comes, you'll probably need at least three nursing bras—one to wear, one for the wash, and one just in case. Regarding size, it's back to the usual routine. The bra should fit properly with the band snug enough around the rib cage that it doesn't ride up your back. As your body shrinks back to normal, you can tighten the band when needed, or you might need to buy a smaller size. There should be a little extra room in the cups to allow for engorgement, and the opening should be big enough for easy access when your hands are full. Look for cotton or

an uplifting update

rebecca's TIP

To protect my breasts from stretching any more than they had to, I wore supportive bras all during my pregnancy and nursing periods, and even slept in softer versions. I'm so glad I did, because after a full course of nursing my son, my breasts maintained their lift and firmness. I also slathered them and my belly with cocoa butters and creams to keep my skin soft and supple. Good for my boy, good for my body!

other breathable fabrics that won't trap moisture against your skin.

Honestly, there are some women who go through their whole maternity and nursing periods without ever wearing bras designed specifically for those purposes. They continue to wear their favorite pretty and sexy bras, just sizing them up. If this sounds more like your style, just make sure to use breast pads to protect both the breasts and the bras.

FIRST BRAS

My tip for buying a young girl her first bra is simple: Be patient. It's a known fact that mothers are a source of endless humiliation to their adolescent daughters, and the embarrassment factor shoots way up when it comes to first bras. If you can, take your daughter to a professional fitter, in an environment that will make it a nice experience. It's bad enough for girls to have their mothers focusing on their breasts, but it's even more traumatizing for some young ladies when there's a salesperson discussing or adjusting their breasts in front of their mothers. But purchasing a first bra doesn't have to be excruciating; it can be fun, educational . . . and very uplifting.

If you feel like you can trust the salesperson, it might be better to step back and let the specialist take care of your daughter, treating her like the grown-up she thinks she now is. While you'll probably be tempted to take a peek in the dressing room, resist the urge. Your daughter may not love being in the hands of a stranger, but it helps demystify the process. She needs to understand that all women have breasts and go through this exciting rite of passage.

If it's not possible to get a professional opinion, exercise patience and compassion. Remember how embarrassing it is for girls, especially the ones who start developing

Her first bra: easing a tween's growing pains.

at eight or nine years old. They're still children, yet they are getting these womanly shapes—it's rough! On the flip side, don't neglect the issue of bras if your daughter is a late bloomer. It's equally embarrassing to be as flat as a board when all the other girls have boys snapping their bras. Can you believe those stale jokes are still circulating around middle school cafeterias about flotation devices and over-the-shoulder-boulder-holders, about mosquito bites and "a pirate's dream: sunken treasure," to say nothing of the dreaded chant that begins "I must, I must . . ."?

Whether your daughter is an early riser or a late bloomer, her first bra should be soft. Not necessarily a soft cup, since she might need an underwire, but it should never be scratchy. Being a teenager is tough enough, but she's off to a bad start if her first bra is uncomfortable. As with anything else in life, a positive first-time experience paves the way for a better future.

A Cautionary Tale
THE TRIALS & TRIBULATIONS OF BOOB JOBS

As you well know, there are a lot of silicone-enhanced boobs populating the planet these days. Most of them greet you before the lady does! While one might think the increase in breast augmentation surgeries would have a significant impact on bra sales, I am here to tell you the contrary. A lot of the women I have encountered who've gone under the knife for these procedures have a difficult time finding attractive bras that fit properly after their surgery.

The problem starts in the plastic surgeon's office, well before surgery, and it usually goes something like this: During a consultation, a woman is shown a series of silicone implants in graduated sizes. She is told that her breasts will end up a certain size based on how many cc's are in the fluid-filled sacs she chooses. Or, sometimes the woman will say she wants to be the same size as so-and-so, not taking into consideration the total physiognomy of the person she wants to look like—that is, her bone structure, body fat content, height, proportions, and all that. A woman is greater than the sum of her parts!

After the swelling has gone down and it's time for the postsurgical visit to a lingerie store, women are often shocked to find that they are much larger in cup size

BEFORE A BUST BOOST

If you are planning to get implants, you can't expect the surgeon to read your mind—it's hard enough to find a hairdresser whose definition of "just two inches" matches yours. Consult a bra expert first to:

- Determine what size you want to be and which styles you want to wear.

- Try on several bras in your normal band size, but with larger cups. Fill the cups with gel inserts to reach your desired size.

- Then, try on clothing similar to what you will most likely wear postsurgery.

Once you've picked your "look," buy a bra in that size and take it, with gel inserts, to your first consultation. Most doctors will try to match your request.

than anticipated. Believe it or not, some of these specialized surgeons are not fully aware of how bras are sized. Bra fitters are continually breaking poor girls' hearts and bursting the bubble on their new boobs.

I had a young lady who was a 32AA preop whose surgeon told her she was going to end up a 34C. "But that's impossible," I thought. Implants increase cup size, but band size remains the same. Going to a 34 from a 32 would mean two inches were added to her rib cage. Now I've heard of surgically removing ribs to get thinner, but who augments a rib cage? Yikes! I had the most difficult time convincing her that her size was, in fact, a whopping 32DDD! Now her breasts sat unnaturally high on her bony chest, and the only bras that fit her new form were matronly full-cup styles.

So why am I telling you this? Because these are the stories you don't normally hear when people talk about breast enhancement. Sure, you learn the obvious risks, the extremes of botched jobs, punctured or leaky sacs, and removal procedures—but let's get practical. People get so excited about the prospect of a brand-new bust that they overlook the issue of what new bras they'll need. It's like buying an enormous couch that doesn't even fit in the door of your studio apartment. Then what do you do? After witnessing many big busts (literally and figuratively), here's a lesson in lingerie that you now won't have to learn the hard way.

Parting Words

The bra is the most complicated, but probably the most important, part of a woman's outfit. It's one of the few articles of clothing that can dramatically alter the shape of your body. Many women see it as a necessary evil, just another hardship we must endure to look our best. Others, like me, consider wearing a bra to be all pleasure, and no pain. It's hard to say that about most relationships! Because when it comes to the fit of your bra, there is no "almost." It either fits or it doesn't. Never settle on the first one you find.

A good bra is hard to find, but there's one (or more) out there waiting for you.

It might mean going home empty-handed at times, but it will be worth it for the right one. A good bra *is* hard to find, but there's one (or more) out there waiting for you.

Brief Encounters

❧ Panties ❧

Panties go by many names. Unlike the bra, which is never called anything else (except "brassiere" by grandmothers who insist on using full names), panties can be underpants, drawers, knickers, or briefs, to name a few. But the very sound of "panty" is titillating, conjuring up associations with words like *dainty, scanty, up the ante,* or even *candy*! From classic schoolgirl briefs to the skinniest of G-strings, panties hold a lot of meaning.

Panties, though less intricate than bras, are much more intimate. From the youngest age, children know there is something a little bit naughty about them. Honestly, does anyone make it to age ten without getting "pants-ed" or giving a wedgie, or being teased about London, France, and her underpants? Designed to protect and cover your privates, undies are tempting because they hide what lies beneath—and, in doing so, bring attention to it. They are a suggestion, but not a promise . . . more of a hint than an answer. When offered like an invitation to a show, panties can be sexually charged, one of the most personal gifts a woman can receive from a lover. Yet underwear can have the opposite effect if it's a present from a parent or a grandparent. "My point? The significance of panties exists in our minds.

You can fantasize about their frivolousness or focus on their simple functionality. Is white cotton innocent, or even more provocative than red lace? It's up to you. **Panties let you choose your own adventure.** Sometimes, when I recall my mother telling me always to wear clean underwear, just in case I had to go to the hospital, I like to turn the picture around. I prefer to imagine the EMTs working all the harder to save me because of my pretty panties—and then maybe even nabbing a doctor in the examining room!

A bra has the power to transform your body by turning molehills into mountains, and mountains into foothills. A pair of panties works its magic in other ways. First, it provides a hygienic and protective barrier between you and possibly scratchy, rough outerwear. Most of its outward importance lies in how it feels and appears under clothing (which is preferably as unfelt and unseen as possible). Panties should be wedgie-free, nonbunching, and breathable. Most important, they should never produce visible panty lines (VPLs). The rest is aesthetics and personal preference, a ticket to putting you in the mood. And not just the mood for love. Panties can make you feel sophisticated (think black lace) or sweet (a ruffly pink confection), sassy (boyshorts) or sexy (thong), innocent (white cotton, of

THE CONTINENTAL DIVIDE

*F*orget about toe-may-toe/toe-mah-toe, there's a vast difference between the U.S. and England when it comes to undies. In America, knickers refers to a type of short pants. Across the pond, knickers are underpants. When Americans talk about pants, they're referring to the outerwear called trousers by the Brits. If the British say pants, they mean underpants.

course) or in control (red satin, with maybe some corset-style lacing). When you reach to the back of your underwear drawer to put on your stretched-out, "I'm definitely not getting any today" undies, to some degree, you've given up from the get-go. It may seem like an overstatement, but in their own little, itty-bitty way, the panties you choose set the tone for the day, or night, ahead. They are your personal understatement.

the lowdown on VPLs

rebecca's TIP

Pssst . . . visible panty lines have been called "VPLs" since the '70s, so if this is the first time you've been downloaded on this code (or haven't been briefed about panty lines in the first place), you might want to look at your bottom in the mirror . . . and then keep reading!

Panty Aid
THE RIGHT FIT

anties might seem like an item you can just grab off a sales rack, but the wrong pair can create lumps and lines that can ruin any outfit. That's why finding the best size and style for you (and your clothing) is so important. Still, many women struggle to find a pair they're happy with. If they're lucky enough to have found a favorite that they undoubtedly want to stockpile, they may find that their one, beloved, tried-and-true style doesn't work under everything (besides, things can get a little monotonous). But judging by the number of unsightly lumps and lines I see in and out of my store, it seems a lot of women aren't willing to face the truth . . . or maybe they can't see behind their backs!

SIZE WISELY

The first issue is sizing. It doesn't matter if you have the most precious little pair of panties in the whole wide world; if they aren't the right size, they're no good.

Luckily, panty sizing is pretty straightforward and standardized. Measure your waist and hips and find the corresponding size.

If you think you're a medium, don't get depressed if you find that large is really the better-fitting size. I know that with bras, even if you get tired of always trying to support your ample bosom, you can take some pleasure from the widespread cultural acceptance (or, shall I say, obsession) with large breasts. In most women's minds, a bigger size isn't always a negative thing. In addition, going down a bra size often means you've lost weight: a win-win situation. On the other hand, panties are a reflection of the size of your rear end, hips, and waist—those parts of our bodies that most of us don't want to get any bigger. Keep in mind, though, that there are plenty of women with less on the backside who would gladly trade in for more in the rear. But none of that matters. What does is that you don't get too stuck on an actual size. *Buy what fits* and, if you really hate that XL tag, cut it out. Nobody will know.

HOW TO JUDGE

There isn't a woman who hasn't worn an uncomfortable pair of underwear at one time or another. I feel like I spent my entire high school years yanking at wedgies that I figured were a necessary evil that came with wearing underpants.

TIGHT TIMES

Q. **Underwear always seems to dig into my legs. I'm pear-shaped, so if I get a bigger size, everything else gets all baggy. Outside of thongs, is there any style that might fit better?**

A. Try going high up or low down. A high-cut leg, designed to keep the entire leg and thigh open and free, avoids the possibility of thigh-binding. Another option? Boyshorts, which offer more bottom coverage and often fall below the problematic cutoff zone.

Waist Measurement	Hip Measurement	Panty Size
23"–24"	33"–34"	4 or XS
25"–26"	35"–36"	5 or S
27"–28"	37"–38"	6 or M
29"–30"	39"–40"	7 or L
31"–32"	41"–42"	8 or XL
33"–34"	43"–44"	9 or 2XL
35"–36"	45"–46"	10 or 3XL
37"–38"	47"–48"	11 or 4XL
39"–40"	49"–50"	12 or 5XL
41"–42"	51"–52"	13 or 6XL
43"–44"	53"–54"	14 or 7XL
45"–46"	55"–56"	15 or 8XL

If you've ever shimmied yourself into an inconspicuous corner in order to reach down the back of your pants to tackle a major wedgie, then you know exactly what I'm talking about when I say that a bad pair of underwear can ruin your day.

Like so many other things in life, when it comes to panties, size isn't everything.

There are many styles—some that sit at your belly button and others that go deep down low, some with a foot of fabric in the back and others with a centimeter of string. The following pointers are general guidelines to help you evaluate the individual elements of your panties—so don't get your knickers in a twist about the actual styles quite yet.

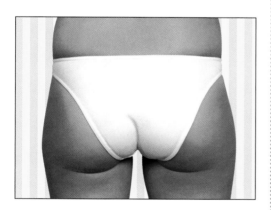

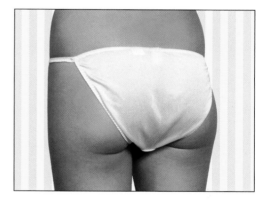

YOUR PANTIES ARE TOO SMALL

1. The waistband on your panties should be comfortably snug. If they're binding or feel tight or create rolls of flab over the waist, go up a size or choose a different cut or style. You can be a total skinny-mini, but too tight band is going to create fleshy overflow on anyone.

2. The same applies to the fit around the legs. If the leg bands are tight enough to make a mark or create a groove, they'll make any saddlebag issues exponentially worse.

YOUR PANTIES ARE TOO BIG

If your panties twist around, bunch up, or generally don't stay put, try a smaller size or another style. There shouldn't be excess fabric. Saggy baggies wrinkle up under clothing, making the rear look bigger. Instead, the back should fit smoothly over the derriere. Coverage is one thing, draping material is quite another.

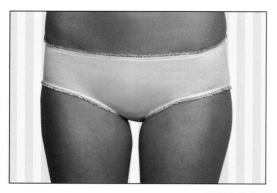

THE PERFECT FITTING PANTY

Your panties should be budgeproof, but not binding, and wedgie-free in the front and back. Except for thongs (or variations, like the Brazilian-cut styles designed to let a little cheek peek out), panties should cover the rear. To protect against wedgies and minimize show-through, look for styles that land almost horizontally underneath the cheeks rather than vertically or diagonally across, so they cup the derriere. This way, your bottom won't be divided into more sections than the two that nature intended. Unless you want to advertise the specific underwear you're wearing, always make sure that none of the panty edges bind your flesh.

WAIST NOT

Q. **I feel like panties dig into my waist and squeeze my love handles. I always end up buying sizes that are too big so this doesn't happen. Are there styles that don't do this?**

A. Look for styles with wider sides that lie flat against your body, rather than string styles that press into hip flesh. If you automatically associate "wide sides" with granny underwear, think again. Since the wide-side look is more popular than strings these days—it's a much more forgiving and flattering look—there are plenty of pretty ones to pick from. (See Panty Shape Update, page 87, for examples.)

VPL ALERT!

I can't say it enough—remember to avoid VPLs. With panties (other than thongs or G-strings), if your rear cheeks are intersected by tight elastic, your visible panty line is there for all to see. It has the same unattractive effect of a too-small bra that cuts a valley across the top of your breasts, creating four unflattering sections. Luckily there are plenty of styles available, because every rear end is different. If you have a boyish figure with not a lot of curve in back, look for a panty with a boy-cut leg. This style is less likely to divide and conquer the

WHAT TO WEAR UNDER THERE

Outside: Tight pants

Inside: Thong or Laser-cut Brief

Wear either a thong or a full-coverage style with seamless edges that won't dig into your flesh. If you're the more adventurous type you can wear nothing at all—but be careful about friction, especially with denim.

wrong

right

rear. For the fuller tush, laser-cut or high-cut styles are best. Like my mother always said, be careful at intersections. In this case, take note wherever fabric ends and skin begins.

What I can't figure out are the women who know that the underwear they're pairing with certain clothing isn't the best match, but who follow some sort of "out of sight, out of mind" theory that makes them believe nobody else notices. Believe me, they notice. It's just that once you're out of high school, it's not too often someone is going to come up to you and blatantly point out your flaws. It's hard enough telling someone she has a poppy seed in her teeth; forget about telling her that her underwear looks terrible. You know how small children hide their eyes and think nobody can see them? Well, the action may be going on

behind you, but everyone else *can* see it, and trust me, it doesn't look good. Baby, watch your back!

LINES OF THE TIMES

Visible panty lines weren't always the fashion faux pas they are today. Until fairly recently, they were accepted as an unfortunate part of life, like wrinkles and body hair. As anthropological evidence, I offer Diane Keaton's character in Woody Allen's ANNIE HALL. I suggest you watch the movie again and notice that the woman immortalized as a gender-bending fashion icon has a serious case of VPLs. Since then our standards of perfection have become much higher—perhaps because we've been numbed to reality by all the airbrushing and liposuction going on. Clothing fits closer than ever now, but mercifully, technological advances have led to fabrics that can seamlessly disappear. And thank goodness the thong has been released from its shady past so that it can be embraced by discerning women everywhere.

Skivvies Shopping

I am sure many of you find that trying on bathing suits is horrifying. There you are, harsh fluorescent lights making every ripple, dimple, and vein jump out. It is an experience to be avoided unless absolutely necessary, like, say, the night before your flight to a tropical island. The exercise of trying on anything on the bottom half is so traumatic to most women that they buy their undies without a test run. And you know what happens? Most of them end up with a drawer full of panties that are too uncomfortable to be worn or, even worse, don't fit but are worn anyway. Are you someone who has only one or two favorites in

> **Imagine reaching into your drawer anytime and having exactly the thing you need.**

your stash—the pairs that give you a sense of security when you know they are clean and waiting? The ones you reach for, then hold off on, thinking you might actually need them even more the next day? You know, the panties you plan outfits and laundry around? Now, imagine if your entire supply of panties was like this pair. You could reach into your drawer anytime and have exactly the thing you need. You wouldn't even think twice because, unless you really let your laundry go, there would be more of the same the next day. This underwear utopia can be yours if only you would try on before you buy.

Yes, I'm saying that you should try on underwear (over your own, naturally). Women often grab handfuls of panties and head to the register at my store. When I suggest they go to the dressing room to try on at least one pair, they look at me like I just asked them to strip naked right there at the counter. What's the big deal? It's one thing if you're buying at a discount store that doesn't have dressing rooms or won't let you try on undergarments, but if you're shopping at a boutique or department store, by all means, try the garment on. Panties are like lipstick: Either you buy it unseen at a drugstore, or you pay more at the cosmetics counter so you can try it out and know what you're getting. Of course, when you try on panties you do have to use your imagination a little bit, since you are putting them on *over*

As anybody who works in a clothing store will attest, we sincerely ask—make that, beg—that all women be freshly bathed before trying on clothes, particularly intimate apparel, and that bottoms should be tried on only over one's own. While you're at it, be careful not to get makeup and deodorant stains on garments—slip things on feet first if possible and wear clear nonresidue antiperspirants. There is nothing ruder than finding an item for sale with signs or scents telling you someone else has been there. The golden rule applies even when in the dressing room: Do unto others' clothing as you would have them do unto yours.

your current pair. Even so, you can get an almost accurate assessment of how they will look. When you know you're going panty shopping, I suggest wearing the most minimal pair you own, preferably a thong. If your current panties are bigger and baggier than the pair you're trying on, in some cases you might want to give them a downward yank so they don't clutter the view.

POINTERS FOR PURCHASING PANTIES

I wish I could say it's easy to get women comfortable in their underwear, but I've seen how freaked out most of you are once you're stripped down to this state. By the time you leave a dressing room, I bet you've spent more time evaluating your body than

the actual panties. Just so you don't feel so alone on your next solo journey into a dressing room, let me share with you a few things I've noticed during the try-on process.

First, most women take the way they look in their skivvies pretty seriously. They also have a tendency to blame themselves for things that don't work out. If you walk into a dressing room feeling perfectly fine, you can't let a bad pair of panties ruin your mood. You might encounter a style that creates flab you didn't even know you had, but just take them off and move on to another, better-fitting pair. Certain styles can create rolls of fat at the hips if that's where you carry weight, but there's another pair that won't make you look that way. And whatever you do, if you walk out happy with your purchase, don't dwell on how you looked in the rejects. That's like remembering an insult but brushing away the compliment!

Another thing: Be open to different styles. Don't dismiss a pair of boyshorts or thongs just because you've never tried them—you might be pleasantly surprised. Once you've got a pair on, you should make sure to evaluate yourself from all angles in the mirror. And *always* check to see what they look like under your clothing, since that's how they will most often be worn.

The Thing About Thongs

Today, the thong is back where it belongs, invisibly fighting VPLs and making private appearances only. The thongs-on-parade style is far from extinct, but the craze has thankfully quieted down. Over the span of less than a decade, or more specifically since the late '90s, the thong went from a provocatively sexual item worn by exotic dancers to a mainstream staple of even the most modest woman's wardrobe. I've overheard many a preteen girl tell her mom, as part of her campaign for a thong, that "everybody at school is wearing them." And she's probably not exaggerating, since thongs are even—and very controversially—made for little girls.

> The thongs-on-parade style is far from extinct, but the craze has thankfully quieted down.

How did a style that is so revealing become so popular? Body-conscious clothing had a lot to do with it. Tighter, clingier fabrics set new requirements for what to wear underneath. Unlike the '80s women who wore pantyhose under their tight black skirts, more recent fashionistas wanted bare legs, and none of the problematic bumps and bulges of traditional panty styles.

But what may have contributed most to the thong's rise to fame was a new focus on the derriere. As the African American and Latin influences on fashion, beauty, and entertainment increased, buttocks became the new breasts. Just think of all the booty-shaking in rap and hip-hop videos, from J.Lo right up to Sisqo's infamous

There's a thong for every occasion.

"Thong Song," which had many women who were previously simply curious about the minuscule garment ready to seal the deal.

In the early days of the twenty-first century, everyone and her mom—literally—were buying thongs. And the phenomenon wasn't that surprising. Underpants have always reflected the cultural climate. If belly button–baring bikinis represented the sexual freedom of the '60s and '70s, the thong was the expression of our contemporary, in-your-face sexuality.

It didn't seem to matter, by the way, if you were toned up and ready to flaunt it, or not quite there yet. The thong showcased all shapes of gluteus maximus beneath equally popular tight, Lycra-

rebecca's tip ▶ bummed out

If you do wear a thong, keep it in your pants. For several years, thongs were like the celebrity you felt you couldn't turn around without seeing everywhere. After the overload of panty-peek, butt-cleavage, and "whale tails" (referring to the fishtail shape of a thong rearing its head above the waistband), you lose the mystery. And call me old-fashioned, but I think girls are wearing far too little, too young. I think it's so much sexier to keep something hidden. Sure, it can be fun to intentionally put on a show-and-tell for a select audience, but do you really need every construction worker on the street to get an eyeful? Far be it from me to act like a prude, but a true coquette doesn't let it all hang out.

infused jeans. Pants were snugger and lower, and more embellished in the rear, to invite special attention to the area. With the low-cut designs, women pushed the envelope by not only wearing thongs, but showing them, too. Of course, it's still taboo to display the pubic region in public, but revealing underwear is the closest thing. If Marky Mark could strip to his Calvins, girls could too!

More recently, better design and fabrications meant thongs got more comfortable than the earlier models, which deserved their reputation of feeling like dental floss. (Actually, once you've found the right thong, you feel as if you're wearing nothing at all.) But after years of the thong thing, the trend reached its saturation point. People were saying "Enough with the thong already!" Women would come to my store and, with a weary look in their eye, ask for "normal panties." However, there are still plenty of ladies who find anything other than a thong uncomfortable.

Thongs continue to thrive, but no longer as a fashion item meant to be displayed for the world to see. They serve a functional purpose under clothing that requires special undergarments. And they'll still put a smile on the face of any guy who is lucky enough to see yours . . . in private, that is.

THONG FIT
Dental Floss Free

Despite their fast rise to fame, thongs carry a stigma—primarily because most women think their derrieres are fat, flat, or flabby. Now, if you've never worn thongs before, you might be afraid that they are too daring, or maybe you simply dread the thought of fabric going up your divide. Diehard thongsters swear they feel fine, but do these ladies protest too much, like the woman squeezed into skyscraper-high stilettos who insists this pair really is comfortable? Part of adjusting to a thong is simply a matter of getting used to it. It's like

wearing a new ring—you might notice it at first, but after a while, you forget it's there. Some styles are more binding and tend to ride up more than others. The most comfortable versions have a flat back panel that lies smoothly against your body (as opposed to a stretchy, rubberbandlike one that pulls up, for that floss feel).

Still, many women like having their tush covered by a pair of briefs; they don't think they have the cheeks for thongs. Since a thong accentuates the two rounds of your rump, any insecurity you might have about your derriere feels exaggerated. For this reason, you may choose to wear thongs out of practicality, but not for anyone to actually see. The truth is, though, most men find thongs sexy. It just triggers something. Monica Lewinsky made thongs famous when word leaked out that she had flashed hers to the president. Women all over the country followed suit (though not necessarily showing theirs to anyone in the Oval Office). Trust me, the very fact that you are in a thong will make any flaws you may obsess about invisible to the guy. Like women, thongs come in all shapes, sizes, and styles. Have a little faith—the perfect fit is out there.

THE STARTER THONG: THE HANKY PANKY 4811

*L*ike a supermodel known by just her first name, this thong is so good people actually ask for it by style number. Responsible for turning many thong virgins into thong addicts, the Hanky Panky comes in three styles—the original cult classic 4811, the low-rise 4911, or the curvy girl 4811X (fits sizes 14–26). All I know is that I refuse to believe anyone who insists that all thongs are uncomfortable unless she has tried this one. Available in a rainbow of colors, it has the ideal combination of comfort and fit. It also looks adorable! If every thong has done you wrong, it's time you get a little hanky panky to treat you right!

THE PERFECT-FITTING THONG

❀ *Supersoft, extra stretchy, nonbinding lace*

❀ *Cotton crotch lining stays where it belongs*

❀ *Lies flat for no show-through or bunching*

❀ *Lightweight (The original weighs in at a mere half ounce; its smaller low-rise sister is one-eighth of an ounce less.)*

hot dates for panties

Pre-1800s

✿ Nice Girls Go Commando

Until the nineteenth century, only men wear underpants. In fact, they are considered scandalous, a sign of looseness. They are for courtesans, not proper ladies!

1800s–early 1900s

✿ Air-conditioned Underpants

Men's drawers get stitched closed at the crotch, but women's are left with an open slit from front to back, mirroring the female anatomy. Called split-knickers or divided britches, these crotchless or bottomless styles allow "easy access" under layers of slips and outer clothing. The question of "open or closed" is a big subject of debate until the turn of the century, and you better believe this makes gentlemen extra attentive to high-kicking cancan dancers.

1807

✿ Panty-peek Preview

James Monroe's daughter, Maria Hester, is said to be the first person to wear pantalettes, a feminine version of pantaloons. Unlike their male counterpart, pantalettes are worn under

clothing, not as pants. Featuring long straight legs ending in tucks, ruffles, and embroidery that show beneath the hem of dresses, they are fashionable for a little more than half a century.

1851 ▲

✿ In Full Bloom

Bloomers, named after Amelia Jenks Bloomer, an American reformer working for healthier dress and women's rights, make their first appearance. This early attempt at sensible dressing is worn as outerwear but is eventually shortened to a form of underwear more closely resembling what we wear today.

1930s

✿ String Theory

Striptease dancers start wearing G-strings, a little bit of artfully placed nothing. The word may come from geestring (adapted from *geestringi*), a loincloth held up by a string and worn by certain American Indians.

1950s

✿ White Out

All the good girls in this era wear pristine panties in pure-as-the-driven-snow white.

1955

✿ More Shocking than a Glimpse of Stocking

When Marilyn Monroe's skirt blows up as she stands over a subway grate in *The Seven-Year Itch*, the whole world learns that it's sometimes what you *don't* see that is really sexy.

1960s

✿ Short and Sweet

No frumpy underpants at Beatles concerts—it's all about bikini briefs under those miniskirts and tight jeans. And, lest you forget, pettipants, those little shorts that come in all sorts of patterns and prints. Girls aren't allowed to wear pants to school, and pettipants make it safe to play sports without revealing it all.

panty shape update ▶

1975

☆ **Thong and Dance**

Designer Rudi Gernreich has been credited with introducing the first thong bikini (as well as the first topless bathing suit). However, some fashion historians trace the first public U.S. appearance of the thong to the 1939 World's Fair, when New York Mayor Fiorello La Guardia ordered that the city's nude dancers cover themselves.

1980s

☆ **Power Undressing**

What goes on beneath those power suits worn to the office

and workout suits worn to aerobics class? The '80s are an age of extremes, during which women take on new roles in society and sports . . . and high-cut legs are the hottest thing. Often referred to as jazz pants, these undies feature legs cut all the way up to the hip bones.

Late 1980s–early '90s

☆ **Getting a Leg Up**

Women wear leggings with everything to look totally smooth. The thong thing begins to emerge, ever so slowly and quietly.

2000

☆ **The Lowdown**

The height of the waistband, known as the rise, dips to an all-time low to fit under lower-than-low-rise jeans.

◀ **2005**

☆ **Girly Boys**

The full-cut boyshort, the skimpy thong's polar opposite, becomes the latest darling to wear downstairs.

When it comes down to it, there are really only five basic panty shapes. From the most material to the least, there's the brief, the bikini, the hipster, the thong, and the G-string. The rest are, more or less, hybrids of these five styles. There are innumerable variations on shape and the names they're called, but from your basic bikini to the more obscure thong boy, it's always good to know your options. Your repertoire should have a little range.

Boyshort/Boy-Leg Brief

A panty style similar in shape to boys' underwear—but much more attractive. Often low in the rise, it has wide sides that hug your hips. Very popular with teens and twenty-somethings because they flatter most youthful body types. Don't fall for the myth that they are universally flattering—they sometimes make legs look shorter and fatter than they actually are. Because of their full-coverage backs, boyshorts usually prevent VPLs. They're great under short skirts and low-slung pants.

panty shape update

 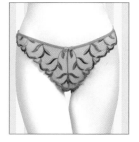

Brazilian Back

A panty style that covers more of the cheeks than a thong, but less than a traditional full-back panty. For a good idea of the cut, think of a Brazilian-style

bikini revealing bronzed beach buns. Not recommended to be worn under thinner clothing, as VPL is guaranteed.

Brief

A panty whose waistband rests at or just below the belly button, provides full back coverage and may, or may not, have high-cut legs. The common connotation

of briefs leans toward a conservative cut or granny pants, but many companies call their sassier boyshort styles "briefs."

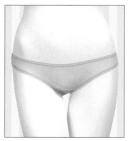 

Low-rise/Hipster/Hip-Hugger

Perfect under low-rise clothing, this style sits at or below the hips. Any type of panty can technically have a low rise, but

if a style is simply called "low-rise," it usually refers to a hipster/boyshort style.

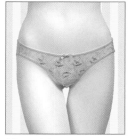 

(String) Bikini

A panty whose waistband rests below the belly button and on the hips. The legs are sometimes high-cut and the

sides can vary from a narrow string to a thick side panel. Back coverage depends on the style of the bikini.

"One should either be a work of art, or wear a work of art."
—OSCAR WILDE

French Knickers

A panty with wider sides and less fabric to cover the bottom of the cheeks, often made of lace, silk, or satin.

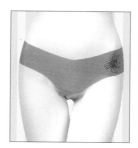

Laser-cut/Seamless

A panty whose edges are cut with a laser to avoid the bulk of stitching and elastic. It provides a completely smooth look; the fewest lines possible today!

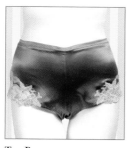

Tap Pant

Feminine, flattering, and sometimes flared, these are sweet and playful shorts, often made of lace, silk, or satin. Think of the shorts worn by tap dancers in days gone by.

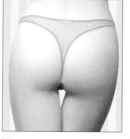

Thong

A style that leaves the buttocks exposed, preventing visible panty lines. Has slightly more fabric than the G-string, but the concept is the same.

T-string/G-string

With even less coverage than a thong, it's a small triangular front panel with a string up the rear and a string around the sides.

Thong Boy

It looks like a panty coming, but a thong going. A cross between a thong and a boy brief, it offers more—but not total—coverage in the back and along the sides, while the cheeks peek out the bottom. A flattering variation on the traditional thong.

PULL SOME STRINGS

Q. **What's the difference between a G-, T-, V-, and Y-string?**

A. Not much, except a letter. Panty naming is not an exact science. All the styles of strings are variations of the same theme.

WHAT TO WEAR UNDER THERE . . . PANTIES

Outside: White linen or cotton pants

Inside: Flesh-colored panties

When you wear white on the outside, you should wear a flesh-colored undergarment underneath—unless you are advertising! A bright, contrasting bra can be a fashion statement, but your panties should not show through. Many women make the mistake of wearing white under white, which creates a bright glowing moon underneath your clothes. Remember, white lies!

Outside: Light summer dress

Inside: Cotton boyshorts

When temperatures are shooting up outside, you want to stay as cool as possible. First off, opt for cotton. Close-

fitting, overly snug underwear can feel like a sticky, sweaty mess, but a pair of cotton boyshorts will keep things easy and breezy, inside and out. If your thighs touch (and most women's do), you can prevent the friction and the constant perspiration this rubbing generates by wearing a stretchy bike short–style panty. I know it sounds counterintuitive to add another layer on a hot day, but it works—no more chafing, no more lumps.

Outside: Thin, silky, or clingy skirt or pants

Inside: Laser cut

Every line shows through a thin fabric, so you need to go seamless. This is not the time to bust out the ruffles, bows, and frills. If you're svelte and firm, wear a thong. Laser-cut panties are also great for

totally clean lines. If your lower half hangs a little too loose for your liking, try control bike shorts—no more cottage cheese! Total smoothness, from waist to hips to thighs.

Outside: Miniskirt or short dress

Inside: Full-cut boyshorts

I like to wear boyshorts or hipsters under a short skirt or dress. In a thong, one false move—or one gust of wind— and it's a total exposé. But pretty bikinis and all forms of girlie boyshorts and briefs let you wear miniskirts with confidence.

WHAT TO WEAR UNDER THERE

Outside: Low-rise jeans or pants
Inside: Low-rise thong or brief

A good rule of thumb is to match the rise of your panties to the rise of your clothing. A low-rise thong is great, but a pair of low-rise briefs can also work, as long as it fits properly and doesn't give you VPLs. Warning: Thongs often sit a little higher than other panty styles and, paired with low-rise pants, can pop up like prairie dogs. If you're not a fan of the plumber's-crack look—and I most definitely am not!—stick with a thong that stays put, or a nice, full-coverage pair of briefs that sits right below your pants' waist.

wrong

right

Panty Problems . . . Solved!

THE COTTON CLUB

When choosing underwear, I recommend investing in natural fibers, since synthetics tend to trap moisture and create a breeding ground for bacteria. Though perspiration and odor are a perfectly normal part of life, I've found certain synthetics can be particularly offensive when it comes to the not-so-fresh feeling. (There's a reason our mothers warned us against sitting around in a wet bathing suit all day!) When you're trying to keep the southern hemisphere healthy and dry, go au naturel with cotton, linen, silk, or even wool. There *are* new synthetic fibers that claim to wick away moisture, but I'm not fully sold on them. Wicking fabric may be okay in the armpits, but things get a little more sensitive below the belt.

Cotton is always comfortable—and it can be chic.

PERIOD PIECES

Let's talk about period pieces (and I don't mean movies based on Jane Austen novels). It's not polite dinner party conversation, but I'm going there anyway: period underwear. We all have it. The sacrificial pairs of panties we put on when it's that time of the month. They're not very pretty, but they are practical. Of course, we don't want to risk ruining our favorite pair, which is why women find it so hard to part with these old chums. Who hasn't put on a pair of these and thought, "This is the last time I'm going to wear these. After I take them off, they're going in the garbage!" . . . and then ended up putting them in the wash and back in the drawer? After all, you figure you can probably get one more wearing out of them.

One of the main problems with this recycling is that stained panties can make you feel even worse than you feel anyway when you get your period. You've totally given up on feeling even close to cute that day. You're dead on arrival. Besides that, they look unpleasant. Most of these pairs are the older ones, and I'll bet they're stretched to the point that they don't even fit properly. I'd also guess that these are the panties that you make sure to ball up and stash at the bottom of your clothes hamper. They're the ones that mortify you when they fall on the floor of the public laundry room. No coquette would be caught in such a situation.

Here's what to do: First, please get rid of those old pairs that I know you have in the back of your drawer. Then, go shopping! Pick up a week's worth of panties that you wear only at that certain time of the month. Go for a dark color like basic black so the slightest spill won't ruin them. Red is also a good option. You can look like a smoldering siren even if you feel like you've been marked with a scarlet letter. Assuming the average period spans a week, including a few days of bloating, crankiness, and maybe some false alarms, that means you spend twelve weeks a year in a "red state."

That's three whole months! This is when you need the positive reinforcement power of nice panties more than ever.

MATERNAL FIGURES: PANTIES

Personally, when I was pregnant, there was no way I was going to be seen in those awful-looking maternity panties you see in catalogs. **The best bottoms for me, believe it or not,** were low-rise briefs or thongs. If you happen to wear this style prepregnancy, then enjoy them even more now, because you won't have to buy specialized underwear for the next nine months. For those who need a little more support while carrying a larger baby or twins, though, there are maternity panty styles that have a special stretch panel woven in the lower abdominal area to help carry the extra load.

Colors and Fabrics

They say the average woman owns fourteen pairs of underwear. I say you should have *at least* that amount and more, since panties are usually less expensive and wear out faster than bras. I often recommend that customers buy two pairs of undies for every bra. If you like matching sets, buy the panty in all the shapes the style is sold in. Get the bikini, brief, *and* the thong to wear under different types of clothing. With panties, you can afford to have some fun with a variety of colors, fabrics, and trimmings. The only real necessity is that you own a nude pair or two that can virtually disappear under white or light-colored clothing. You should also have something seamless for those thin or silky fabrics where seams will otherwise show through. As I mentioned before, one thing that you should always seek out in underwear is a crotch made from cotton or other natural fiber. Unless it's a novelty item, don't buy underwear with a synthetic crotch. It can be fine, but good old-fashioned cotton is the safest bet.

> I often recommend that customers buy two pairs of undies for every bra. Get the bikini, brief, and the thong.

A bra is best with multiple panty partners.

A lot of women, stuck on the same styles they always wear, balk at some panty options. They say things like, "No, I don't think so. It's just not me." While it's important to feel comfortable, don't be afraid to buy panties that are a little out of character. It's one thing if you think something is flat-out ugly, but you don't want to wear the exact same kind, day in and day out, for the rest of your dreary lingerie life. Change it up!

WARM THE MONEY

Florenz Ziegfeld, the great showman behind the Ziegfeld Follies, is reputed to have dressed his chorus girls in extravagantly expensive undergarments. When a financial backer questioned him about the cost of these underthings which no one would see, he replied that the girls would know they were wearing them, and it would influence how they moved.

Date Panties, Daily Panties

Most single girls wear their nice panties when they are going out on a date. In fact, they often buy new ones. Wearing pretty undies shouldn't depend solely on the hope that someone else will see them. Sure, I can't deny it's much more fun when there's someone to enjoy the view, but what happens when you're in a rut, having a dry spell, or just feeling blah? I know a girl who swore that every time she went out thinking something might happen, it never did. Each time she shaved her legs and moisturized and carefully picked out her panties to fit in with her perfectly orchestrated plan for how the evening would turn out, nothing happened The times when she wasn't prepared, when she wasn't expecting anything, were when she'd somehow find herself making excuses to avoid revealing her scratchy legs or ugly undies. Like a good Girl Scout, you need to be prepared. You don't have to wear over-the-top sexpot numbers every day. I'm just saying, wear something you wouldn't be humiliated to be seen in. You never know when an opportunity might present itself. If you hoard your pretty little pairs for some future occasion, they might never see the light of day. Put them into the daily, or at least monthly, rotation. If you build it (and by "it," I mean a pretty and practical panty collection), they will come.

> **Wearing pretty undies shouldn't depend solely on the hope that someone else will see them.**

Underwear is meant to be worn, not saved.

Slip into Sleep

🌹 Slips & Sleepwear 🌹

You wouldn't get very far if you tried to walk down the street wearing even the most demure bra and panty set with nothing else on but a pair of shoes. And while shapewear can be passed off as exercise gear, it's not something most women want to reveal that they're wearing *under* their clothes, much less advertise out in the open. Slips, chemises, camisoles, and nightgowns, however, do double duty, working both as beautiful underwear and sexy, hip outerwear.

It wasn't always so. Not very long ago, the role of lingerie was clear, much like the role of women themselves. There were set definitions in terms of what was worn when, why, and where. But over the decades, society, like a lover undoing the lacing on a corset, has slowly loosened the rigid requirements for proper dressing.

Now it's hard even to tell if something is a slip or a dress. Camisoles are as much hot little tops for wearing out as they are *under*things to keep concealed—yet more proof of the blending and blurring of the boundaries between what was once strictly unmentionable and is now visible everywhere.

Loungewear . . . or Everywhere Wear

As other items that were once kept strictly under wraps came out, new types of sleepwear emerged in the form of loungewear. After sporting some form of uniform all day on the job, people wanted to relax. T-shirts (especially oversize castoffs from boyfriends), sweats, leggings, boxer shorts, and tank tops were often the items of choice, put on immediately after arriving home and often not taken off until it was time to leave for work the next day.

In addition to T-shirts, yoga wear and other sporty, stretchy styles became a key part of the casual loungewear lifestyle. Sleepwear was no longer just for sleep, but rather all-purpose outfits for the nights and weekends, versatile enough to wear while curled up on the couch watching television, reading in bed, sleeping in, and then wearing to the gym the next morning. On the weekends, it could extend to twenty-four-hour dressing, with the same comfortable clothes worn for shopping and running errands.

Even though I own a lingerie store that is popular with the most style-conscious people, young and old, I can't help but feel old-fashioned when I talk about "kids these days." Teenagers wear their pajama pants everywhere! And while wearing jammies is as comforting as a security blanket, there's still something a little overly relaxed about high school– and college-age girls traveling through airports in pajama bottoms or boxer shorts. They're like little Hugh Hefners, someone who has made the round-the-clock pajama trend his signature look for half a century. Hef asserted his role as the king of his castle by wearing pajamas morning, noon, and night—an "I don't have to answer to anyone" mind-set that most adults with a boss could never get away with. But while silk pajamas and smoking jackets symbolize the ultimate life of leisure and luxury, not bothering to get dressed is more like a life of slovenliness. **As much as I like to get undressed when I'm staying in, I never forget to get dressed when I'm going out!**

I believe there's a real mental benefit to coming in the door and removing your

I think baggy, oversize T-shirts are the most unattractive things a woman can put on at the end of the day. I may be in the minority here, but why anyone would want to look like a formless sack of potatoes is beyond me. How does a woman ever expect to get any attention in one of those unflattering rags? Frankly, you'll never find me lounging about in a boyfriend's old T-shirt. Never! Men's T-shirts are boxy and meant for men. Instead of his, I'll wear my own, thank you very much, because if I'm going to wear a T-shirt, you better believe it's going to be cut to show off my assets. If it's that loose, breezy, relaxed feeling you like, there are so many more beautiful options that make you feel feminine, pampered, and good about yourself. Trust me, I'm the queen of comfort!

Ladies who lounge can be casual, comfortable—and sophisticated.

street clothing—however stretchy and soft it might be and however much you don't feel like changing. It's like a costume change that helps you move to the next scene, allowing you to leave the chaos of the outside world behind. Likewise, I think it's equally important to put on sleep clothes before you hit your bed. Here's why: Too many people spend their final moments before drifting off to sleep making a mental to-do list for the next day, and then remembering what they forgot to do earlier. No wonder we have an insomnia epidemic! I'm here to help. Reduce your caffeine intake. Don't drink too many liquids before bed-

time. And then change into a garment made especially for the purpose of sleeping. The nightly ritual helps turn your bedroom into a private sanctuary, meant for the sole purpose of rest and rejuvenation, or other pleasurable pursuits. Besides the physical comfort of a nice clean nightie or pair of pajamas (which won't bring the grit and grime of the streets in as a strange bedfellow), putting them on is like a grown-up lullaby, sending a soothing psychological message that it's now time to rest.

Just as babies should never be put in their cribs for discipline, but only for sleep, we big babies need the same separation between day and night. If you're someone whose bed also serves as couch, home office, and dining table, don't be surprised if it's harder to shut down when you lie down.

In case you haven't caught on by now, I don't think it's particularly generous to wear your oldest, most beat-up clothing around the house (unless maybe you're painting it). Why reserve the rejects for yourself and your loved ones and save your special, dolled-up side only for strangers, coworkers, or special occasions? You don't need to strut around the kitchen in heels and full makeup (on a regular basis, that is), but it's just as easy to wear something that's comfy and pretty as something that's tattered and unattractive. That's why I'm thrilled to see the beginnings of a backlash to the casual sleep-to-street styles. People are starting to look for things that are worn only in the privacy of their homes and bedrooms, such as sleepwear intended for sleeping in and loungewear meant truly for lounging. I couldn't be happier.

It was 1966, and an orange hip-hugger bell-bottom pajama and bra set was just the thing.

BARE FACT

The Pajama Name The word *pajama* is Hindustani, derived from the Persian words *pa* (which means "leg") and *jama* (meaning "a garment").

pajama party

Bed Jacket

A short jacket meant to be worn over a nightgown for warmth and coverage around the boudoir, in bed while recovering from an illness, or, for the lucky ladies, while eating breakfast in bed.

Short Nightgown

A short and sweet number for slumber, often made of cotton or other light material. Also known as a "nightie."

Tailored Pajamas

Any simple pajama set that is not overly decorated. Reminiscent of men's tailored garments and sometimes finished with piping.

Babydoll

A short, flowing empire nightgown, usually with a matching panty bottom. Originally made of sheer fabric with short puffy sleeves, it now describes many styles of short, swingy (and often sexy) sleepwear.

Long nightgown

A long bias-cut gown that is sliplike but intended for sleeping and lounging, not for wearing as a liner under outerwear. It's for beneath the covers, not beneath clothing!

pajama party

Shortie Pajamas ▶

Two-piece pajamas with short bottoms, most often worn in warm weather.

◀ Peignoir

A feminine robe in an elaborate or sheer fabric; usually found with a matching nightgown, as part of a peignoir set. The name is derived from the French meaning "to comb," because the style was originally worn while combing the hair those one hundred strokes.

Loungewear

Dressed-up two-piece pajamas for wearing around the house. An elegant alternative to a T-shirt and sweatpants.

Chinese Pajamas

Designed after garments worn in China, this style pairs pajama pants with a mandarin jacket featuring side slits and, often, braided front closures called frogs.

◀ Nightshirt/Nightshift

An elongated shirt worn for sleeping, modeled after a man's shirt or a poet's shirt, as is pictured here, with a rounded hem and slits in the side seams. In the mid-1980s, T-shirt and tank variations made for women started doubling as daywear.

Kimono/Kabuki Robe ▶

A robe modeled after the Japanese kimono with wide sleeves, often with a floral or scenic print, and closed with buttons or frogs, or a belt. A kabuki robe is a short version of the same, and is closed with a sash.

Bathrobe

Usually made of terrycloth or waffle-weave cotton for throwing on after bathing. Think of a giant towel with sleeves.

◀ Negligee

A flowing robe made of delicate, often diaphanous fabric and featuring lace and ruffles. Often worn with a matching nightgown.

◀ Teddy

Once made of silk or the like, it combines a tap pant and cami. Teddies can be flowing or fitted, stretchy or slinky, with or without underwires, full coverage or thong-back. Ruffly versions are meant for play, but a teddy can be an undergarment (see page 109).

from sleep to street *STARS IN THEIR UNDERWEAR*

1930s ▼

✿ **Carole Lombard, Marlene Dietrich, Greta Garbo**

Hollywood starlets wear long dressing gowns and bias slips, which were introduced in the 1920s. They become extremely popular in the '30s and remain a classic to this day.

Jean Harlow

1934 ▶

✿ **Claudette Colbert, IT HAPPENED ONE NIGHT**

Spoiled heiress Ellie Andrews (played by Colbert) runs off to escape her family . . . and into Clark Gable. Forced to share a motel room, she borrows his pajamas, starting a trend that is copied across the country. Another fashion phenom from the movie occurs after Gable famously takes off his dress shirt to reveal a bare chest. Men across America are shocked to find that Clark Gable doesn't wear an undershirt—but if he doesn't, why should they? Sales of undershirts plummet about 75 percent, devastating the underwear industry. It literally happened one night!

1951–1957

✿ **Lucille Ball, I LOVE LUCY**

Lucy, who gets herself into all sorts of sticky situations trying to become an obedient stay-at-home wife, often wears men's-style pajamas like those worn by her husband, Ricky, whose career she envies.

1954 ▶

✿ **Grace Kelly, REAR WINDOW**

Who could forget the nightgown? Kelly, playing the fashion editor

girlfriend of laid-up, commitment-phobic photographer James Stewart, pulls a frothy pale pink floor-length confection (with matching satin slippers) out of her strictly business attaché case in Alfred Hitchcock's legendary film. She wants to get married; he likes his semisolitary life (and spying on the neighbors). The moment

that nightgown *floats* out of that case, the battle lines are clear: the flag of femininity is being waved in his private bachelor pad.

1956

✿ **Carroll Baker, BABY DOLL**

A full-on fashion trend starts when Miss Baker sashays across the screen in a short nightgown—a style eventually named after the movie. Considered risqué at the time, the film is condemned by the Legion of Decency as "evil in concept" for its "carnal suggestiveness," certain to "exert an immoral and corrupting influence on those who see it." After being canceled in over 75 percent of its scheduled theaters and lambasted by *Time* magazine, the movie is finally approved by the Production Code Administration. The babydoll remains extremely popular into the '60s, whether it's worn by Samantha in *Bewitched* or the wacky go-go dancing Goldie Hawn on *Laugh-In*.

1958
☆ **Elizabeth Taylor,** CAT ON A HOT TIN ROOF
The slip plays a starring role in Maggie's attempts to regain the affections of her husband, Brick, played by Paul Newman. That image of her leaning in the doorframe is forever implanted in the imagination (see page 107). Now those are the cat's pajamas.

1960 ▲
☆ **Janet Leigh,** PSYCHO
Leigh's appearance in the beginning of the film wearing a white bra and half-slip

symbolizes goodness; she later wears the same lingerie ensemble in black after events take a dark turn. (Although half-slips are tame by today's standards, they were a radical departure from their longer predecessors when introduced in the 1940s.) Leigh's lingerie is bought off the rack, not made-to-order, because Hitchcock wants women viewers to identify with the character.

1965
☆ **Julie Christie,** DARLING
Sleepwear moves out of the bedroom, at least as far as the living room, and is worn for entertaining or hanging about the house. Caftans, robes, and printed pajamas are a key part of that '60s and '70s bohemian hostess look—and make it to the Academy Awards when Julie Christie wears gold PJs to accept her Oscar for *Darling*.

1967 ▶
☆ **Anne Bancroft,** THE GRADUATE
What says seduction more clearly than Mrs. Robinson's leopard-print slip and bra? In the '60s, young women start abandoning the complex undergarments of their mothers, but it's clear that Benjamin, the bumbling college

grad, is used to seeing girls his age in something less mature, like simple cotton. Prints show up everywhere in the ubiquitous nylon tricot.

1986
☆ **Kim Basinger,** 9½ WEEKS
In an erotic movie that epitomizes '80s excess, Basinger's character wears some sexy things under her power suits. Women of the period have better jobs and more money, and spend it on luxurious camisoles, lace teddies, bodysuits, and all forms of frilly things.

1990
☆ **Demi Moore,** GHOST
In the late '80s, women didn't just sleep *with* their boyfriends, they slept *in* their boyfriends' oversize T-shirts and boxers. Demi Moore makes the perfect nod to the trend toward androgyny when she puts on her dead husband's T-shirt in *Ghost*.

1990s
☆ **Courtney Love and Drew Barrymore**
Now that underwear is "outed," fashion-forward women start wearing slips for evening and day wear. Many find them at vintage stores,

since all the lovely, lace-trimmed, classic styles have virtually disappeared off the retail radar. (If stores stocked slips, they were usually more utilitarian, simply cut and made of synthetic fibers in various shades of beige, black, and white.) Designers see the crossover appeal and start modeling their collections after lingerie, creating flimsy, flowing, slighter styles of dresses.

2006
☆ **Naomi Watts,** KING KONG
What's old is new again—not just in movies, but in fashion—as Watts wears a traditional slip in the remake of this classic flick.

The Long and Short of It

The slip has recently slipped back into style. Not the slip dress, but the slinky, silky garment worn under clothes and behind closed doors. I have always stood behind slips, keeping my own private label in stock during the '90s and early 2000s, when everyone was wearing them as dresses. Well, let me tell you, honey, they are back! Slips are once more an around-the-house staple.

> **Slips are once more an around-the-house staple.**

In the movie *Unfaithful,* Diane Lane wore a black La Petite Coquette slip in a steamy scene with her husband, Richard Gere. Personally, I think the slip played just as much a role as the actors themselves! It reminded me why I love a good old-fashioned slip. It is such a classic, elegant form of sleepwear. Where everything else has been reduced to boobs and butts, the slip takes the entire body into consideration. It is understated, subtly seductive, mildly suggestive, inciting the imagination to run wild. A slip doesn't reveal much, but it sure can tease with a strategically placed slit to show off some leg, or delicate lace here and there to shadow décolleté. But perhaps the most exciting property of the slip is that it is one single item, held up by the thinnest of straps—the slightest brush on the shoulders can send it sliding to the floor.

I almost always wear slips at home. It makes me feel like Liz Taylor in *Cat on a Hot Tin Roof* (which is especially fitting because my apartment, like many in Manhattan, is so hot that I need to open the window in the middle of winter). As opposed to a T-shirt, a slip falls and drapes over a woman's body, creating a silhouette that is

A classic, almost conservative silk slip is a little black dress undressed. In Unfaithful, *Diane Lane smoldered in her simple, sumptuous slip . . . from La Petite Coquette, of course.*

distinctly feminine. I also like prancing around in chemises, which fall only to the thigh, and camisoles with tap pants. These sassy little ensembles are often more playful than the sophisticated sister item, the slip.

Even grander than the slip, though, are gowns, arguably the most glamorous of all sleepwear creations. (I'm not talking about the up-to-the-neck cotton and flannel ones your grandma wore.) Hollywood heroines of the 1930s adorned themselves with long, lavish nightgowns fashioned like bias-cut evening gowns. Today, people seek out these vintage treasures to wear as wedding dresses or evening wear, while some of the hottest designers copy them for their couture lines. Such gowns, with matching peignoirs, are also often (and obviously) bought by brides to be worn on their honeymoons, but sadly, the first time they are worn is usually also the last. When the honeymoon is over, the beautiful nightgowns get packed away, stored as keepsakes along with the actual wedding gown. Why is this? Every bride is a little bummed out that she can wear her Vera Wang only once, but there's no reason to relegate the nightgowns to the storage unit too.

By the way, don't feel compelled to adhere to the tradition of wearing white on the wedding night if it's not really your style. Anyway, a gown in a deep, vivid color is more wearable around the house, where it might be exposed to the hazards of coffee stains and, in time, children's sticky fingers. Furthermore, if you think of yourself as a practical type who's not up for any fluff, keep in mind that gowns come in many lengths—you don't have to go with sweeping, floor- length satin and silk to look ravishing. A simple, sleek, below-the-knee slip is gorgeous without being at all froufrou. It's up to you. But believe me, nightgowns are truly something special; every woman should have a matching gown and robe hanging somewhere in her closet or carefully stashed in her drawer. Don't let it collect dust and wrinkles—wear it

Liz Taylor in Cat on a Hot Tin Roof.

to remind you that you're an empowered, confident woman in touch with her femininity.

Mind you, not everyone wears sleepwear. When Marilyn Monroe was asked what she wore to bed, she is rumored to have said, "Chanel No. 5." Some people like to feel nothing between them and their high-thread-count sheets. Even still, it's nice to have that slip nearby in case you need some quick coverage. Not even I like running around the house in the buff!

REBECCA'S TIP ▶ multitasking

My favorite style of slip, with spaghetti straps and a just-below-the-knee length, not only does the trick for a romantic, who-knows-where-the-night-will-lead evening, but also works as a liner under a clingy or see-through dress. In fact, tucked into a skirt, a pretty one with decent coverage can impersonate a camisole.

getting the slip YOUR SLIP WARDROBE

When most people think of a slip, a simple silhouette usually comes to mind, but slips come in all sorts of shapes and styles. Take a look and find the perfect thing to wear under both your clothes and the covers. With these models on hand, you'll have most of your fashion requirements covered.

Full Slip

Worn under sheer dresses to reduce transparency or under unlined dresses, this item prevents clinging and provides smoothness. You should have a plain slip in a flesh color to wear under sheer garments, another simple slip in black or another color, and one lacy slip for fun.

Pantliner

Also known as an underliner, this pantaloonlike garment is worn with unlined pants to protect your skin from scratchy fabric, to prevent your garment from stretching or clinging, and to reduce transparency under sheer pants.

Chemise/Shift/Smock

A slip that hangs straight to a place somewhere on the thigh, it is usually not fitted to the body.

Teddy

Originally, in the 1920s, the teddy was more like a camisole with a straight, nonflared short slip bottom that included a wide strap attached to the front and back hem to make separate openings for each leg. When it was brought back into fashion, it was (and still is) more like a bathing suit—a tight-fitting, one-piece number with either high-cut legs or a thong back.

Half-slip

These serve the same purpose as a full slip under unlined skirts or dresses, but start at the waist. You should have half-slips in varying lengths ranging from mid-thigh to above-the-knee to midcalf.

Bias Slip

A slip whose fabric is cut on the diagonal for a flattering fit. (The hem is still parallel to the floor.) The closer fit means the slip moves with you without binding or pulling.

BARE FACT

Bandeau Slip/Strapless Slip/Bra-slip
Essentially a slip with a fitted top, this hybrid became popular in the 1960s and has been worn ever since under strapless dresses.

WHAT TO WEAR UNDER THERE

Outside: Clingy knit dress or skirt

Inside: Silky slip

If the knit fabric sticks to your skin and tends to bunch up, wear a silky slip in either a full or half style. Smooth and slippery, it will prevent static and keep the skirt moving with you, rather than against.

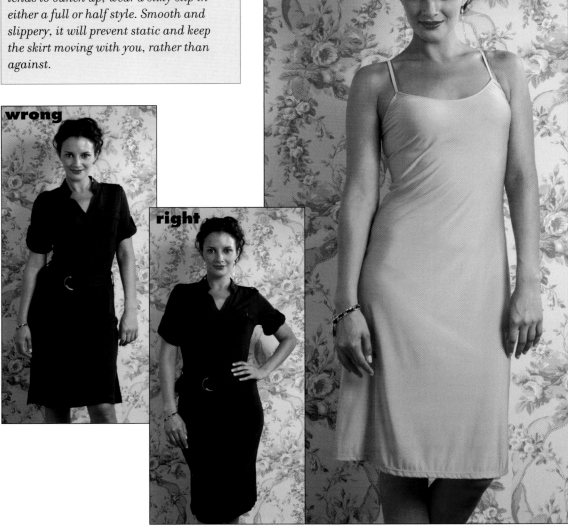

A Plea for a Private Life

*I*nstead of jumping into your yoga gear after a grueling day, consider sliding into something more luxurious. For a while it was nice that intimate apparel wasn't so compartmentalized and you could wear anything anywhere, but we've lost something along the way. Sure, you can roll out of bed and roll out the door and roll around town in the same thing you woke up in. But more women are realizing that there is life (and lingerie) beyond a pair of stretchy black pants and a giant T-shirt. We like to be able to answer the door for a delivery or run out to the store without having to change, but a pretty slip or nightie, strictly for inside wear, keeps something sacred. It invites you to reclaim your private life, a world either for your eyes only, or for those you choose to share it with.

It invites you to reclaim your private life, a world either for your eyes only, or for those you choose to share it with.

Remember, if the postman comes over, you can always throw on a robe—or take it off! Sometimes, when we feel like we're always going, going, going, it's nice to wear something that says **"Oh, no,** I'm definitely staying home tonight."

You don't have to be a starlet to strike a pose.

What Lies Beneath

❧ Shapewear ❧

latter stomach. Smaller waistline. Narrower hips. Perkier bottom. Thighs that don't jiggle or wiggle. While lingerie can't make you instantaneously drop two dress sizes (well, maybe one), the right shapewear can improve almost every figure flaw a woman might think she has. It can smooth, slim, push in, pull up, control, and contour, making it possible for women of all ages to wear clothing that

positively shows off body features they'd otherwise rather not flaunt. In other words, do you want to wear that slinky dress but can't because of a bulging belly or surplus saddlebags? Then shapewear (also known as bodyshapers) may be for you. Indeed, it's for any woman who cares more about looking good *in* her clothing than out of it. It may not be pretty (some of it is), but it sure is practi-

cal. (Although the corset was also intended to reshape the body to look better in clothes, it held a sex appeal all its own. It's hard to say that about contemporary shapewear, which can sometimes look like a costume designed for a '50s B movie about outer space.) And as long as women wear clingy, body-hugging clothing, they will continue to buy products that make them look a little sleeker and

Madonna shaped a generation by rocking foundations—and foundation garments.

leaner in all the right places. The appropriate shapewear can transform a flabby body into a firm and fit form instantly. I see it every day.

Women who've discovered the benefits of shapewear love the effect. It's perfection without detection—a friend who stands by you as you get older, settle down, or have children. Even as the average national weight moves rapidly away from the impossibly long, lean, and lithe idealized female figure, shapewear is poised to meet the

demand. Particularly now that it looks as if most of us may have our stay extended another decade or so—thirty is the new twenty, but ninety is the new seventy—our bodies don't always get the memo. Shapewear steps in as a welcome solution, when it's not quite time to hang up the hat (or tight dress) on looking good.

When most women think of the buckled and bound girdles of the past, they say, "Thank goodness I didn't live then." It's a relief that styles have changed. But there's a problem: We're expected to wear tight, formfitting clothing without any help from what our grandmothers would have called "foundation garments." No wonder so many women are relying on their local plastic surgeon to do the tucking and reducing that underwear used to provide. **Instead of altering our clothing, we're often more apt to alter ourselves.**

I'm here to tell you: Before you go under the knife, visit your local lingerie store.

Many shapewear items have names that include words such as *toner* and *control*—implying all the gain (minus the pain) of hours spent at the gym, and making some women view shapewear as an easier alternative to exercising or dieting. One company goes so far as to describe its product as

"Liposuction Without Surgery." Well, I wouldn't go that far. But even if you do work out—and I hope you do—you'll probably continue to have some soft or saggy parts. We're women! If the cellulite doesn't get you, gravity eventually will—no matter how slim or toned you are. It's a relief to know there's another *comfortable* way to trim the thighs and tighten the tummy at the times we need it most.

I know we all want to look as perfect as the celebrity du jour. And we can. For while we lack the entourage of personal trainers and stylists—to say nothing of photographic retouchers—we do have access to that behind-the-seams accomplice to all those red-carpet looks. Surprise: It's shapewear. I won't mention any names, but I've sold enough shapewear to stars to promise you it's what you don't see underneath those Oscar gowns that gives that mind-boggling, gravity-defying va-va-voom. Shapewear lets you fake it so you don't have to shake it.

Shaping Up

We've come a long way from the constricting garments of yesteryear that made fainting couches necessary—or even from the girdles worn as recently as the '60s that left behind red, swollen welts. Unlike their predecessors that squeezed flesh so tightly they bordered on bondage, modern styles are breathable and flexible. That's because today's shapewear gets its strength from a combination of sophisticated weaving techniques and elasticity. But in general, the more spandex—and it can range from about 5 to 39 percent—the more support, compression, and control you get. (To put

> **Unlike their predecessors that squeezed flesh so tightly they bordered on bondage, modern styles are breathable, flexible.**

those percentages in perspective: The average pair of stretch jeans contains about 2 percent spandex.) What's really significant, though, is that today's designs integrate the control in the fibers of the garment for a more even distribution of powerful support and increased comfort, with fewer bumpy, irritating seams, buckles, hooks, ties, and zippers. In fact, they often have no closures at all!

CONTROL ISSUES

Though the control level is occasionally marked on the label (light, moderate, or firm), it's hard to tell how an item will shape up on you without actually putting it on. You can also explain to a knowledgeable salesperson what you're looking for—even if you don't know the specific item, you most likely have a pretty clear idea of the end result you're trying to achieve—and she may steer you in the right direction. Still, you should try it on.

If you are determined to go by the labels—and don't say I didn't warn you—here are some general ideas of what you can expect. The lighter end of the spectrum will smooth, but won't reshape your body; think of a regular pair of leggings or tights. When you wear an item with moderate control, expect it to tone your body (think control-top pantyhose), but it won't necessarily reduce your size. Firm control can take off centimeters by slightly flattening the tummy, whittling the waist, and/or slimming the hips and thighs, all with

DRESSING ROOM TIP

I often tell my customers to bring with them the garment they want to wear over the control item. There's no better way to tell the final outcome than by giving it a dress rehearsal in the dressing room.

evenly distributed compression (no tourniquetlike strangulation). The elastic memory fibers that make up these garments stretch enough so you can slip them on without much difficulty, then recover quickly to mold to your body for incredible control and shaping.

wedding worries   **rebecca's TIP**

When it comes to buying the things you will wear under your bridal gown, my advice is this: First, have an idea of what kind of dress you want to wear, and then go try on the appropriate underwear for that style. It's a crucial step in the process of choosing a wedding gown. Bring the undergarments that flatter you and make you feel the most confident and beautiful to that first dress fitting. I know from firsthand experience that it will save you many a teardrop. I can't tell you how many times I've witnessed eleventh-hour bridal meltdowns because there was no bra, corset, or panties suitable for the wedding dress that was already purchased.

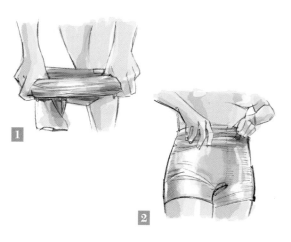

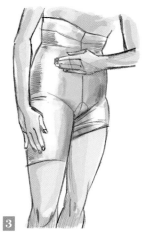

GETTING IT ON

In days gone by, control garments were so stiff and heavy that putting them on was a feat in itself. You couldn't even do it yourself. Then, after being squeezed in, you nearly suffocated from the pressure. Not so anymore. The advent of spandex lets you pull the pieces on and off with ease, using the same technique you use to put on pantyhose.

1. Gather the legs so that you can hold the entire garment bunched in your fingers.

2. Step into both leg holes and pull the fabric up to the place where you want the shaping to start.

3. Then, unroll the garment upward, making sure not to twist it as you go, until it is fully stretched over your body.

4. Smooth it out in every direction. Now everything should be where it belongs.

THE RIGHT FIT

Waiting to exhale? You shouldn't be. Once you properly put on the garment, it should be relatively comfortable—not something you want to tear off your body immediately. You know how when the doctor takes your blood pressure, she pumps up the armband just to the point of discomfort? You shouldn't reach that level of compression.

If it feels comfortable, the first things you should check are the edges. Make sure your skin doesn't bulge where the edges of the fabric meet your body. You'll never get a smooth look under clothing if the garment simply displaces the problem bulges to other locations. It will look bad, and the tourniquet effect will be uncomfortable.

Now take it for a test-drive. Sit, stand, bend over, and walk around a bit to see if the garment stays put. If it shifts around immediately, you know that it's going to be a persistent problem—and one that will be mighty difficult to adjust in public. Think about wearing it for several hours: Do you think you'll be comfortable? Sometimes we justify a pair of painful shoes by saying they just need some breaking in. We know that such optimism most often doesn't work, and with shapewear, it never works—what you see is what you get. If it's no good in the beginning, it never will be.

Manage your assets with power panties.

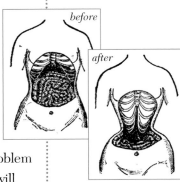

before

after

hot dates for shapes

▼▲ 16th Century to 1914

☆ Straitlaced

A small waist has epitomized youth and beauty since the mid-sixteenth century. During the Victorian period, women are so tightly corseted they suffer attacks of "the vapors" from not being able to breathe, much less bend over. Lack of mobility is a status symbol that means a woman is rich enough to be idle.

1920s

☆ Bound for Glory

The androgynous, flat-chested flappers of the '20s are an aberration, a blip in the centuries-old idolatry of a female form with exaggerated secondary sex characteristics achieved by any means necessary. Not everybody breathes a sigh of relief, though. Women with curves bind their breasts and behinds in order to wear the straight shift dresses of the day. The style is definitely more about boyish bobs than girlish boobs!

1930s ◀

☆ Curves Ahead

Women wear corsets to get the curvy shapes of Jean Harlow, Greta Garbo, and Marlene Dietrich. And let us not forget Vivien Leigh: It took no small feat of corsetry to achieve Scarlett O'Hara's legendary eighteen-inch waist in *Gone With the Wind*.

1950s ▶ ▶

☆ The Hip Girls

Inspired by the hourglass figures of cleavage icons such as Jane Russell, Marilyn Monroe, Sophia Loren, and Elizabeth Taylor, women squeeze themselves into corselets and girdles. By squeezing the waist, both boobs and hips emerge.

1951 ▼
☆ **Widow of Opportunity**
Inspired by a film of the same name starring Lana Turner, the Warner company introduces the "merry widow," a bra joined to a short elasticized girdle (sometimes with garters attached for stockings).

1960s
☆ **Good-bye to Grandma's Girdle**
During an era of joyful rebellion, all types of constrictive underwear are thrown out, and pantyhose take the place of a girdle and stockings. The "swinging '60s" lives up to its nickname in all ways.

1970s
☆ **Fitness Frenzy**
The dance and exercise craze that emerges late in the decade has a huge influence on the refinement of foundation wear. Even before the movie *Saturday Night Fever* comes out, women are wearing leotards with tight jeans or flowing skirts to discos. They become accustomed to wearing smooth stretchy sports gear that shows off their hard-earned hard-bodies. What follows is the realization that those same Lycra-heavy fabrics can help make any body look more toned.

Late 1970s
☆ **Just Don't Say Girdle**
When phrases like "shapewear" and "bodyshapers" come around, they are merely euphemisms, since these garments essentially serve the function of the girdle . . . but without the old-fashioned (and uncomfortable) connotation. By the late '70s the girdle is more or less an antique, replaced with the much more comfortable, modern shapewear we know and love (or loathe, depending) today!

1980s
☆ **Material Girls**
Madonna reincarnates foundation garments, but in forms never before seen—starting with her "Like a Virgin" white lace outfit with a bustier top and crinoline bottom, then in her black bra and sheer lace top ensembles in the film *Desperately Seeking Susan,* and culminating in the infamous Jean-Paul Gaultier corset with cone-shaped cups during her "Blonde Ambition" tour in 1990. While corsets may have disappeared as an undergarment, they resurface as a piece of outerwear. Suddenly, Madonna wannabes begin wearing modified versions of the icon's stage costumes—pairing all variations of unmentionables with jeans and skirts.

1990s to 2000s
☆ **Flattery Will Get You Everywhere**
Under tight clothes even trim, toned bods benefit from support and shaping—but these stretchy and sporty "foundation garments" owe more to exercise clothes than corsetry.

the many shapes of shapewear

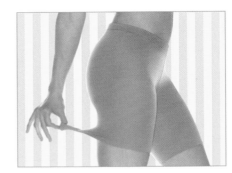

Control Briefs, Thongs, Shorts, Long-leg Panties or Pants Liners

Control Briefs

A brief, available in various lengths, made with elastic yarns designed to smooth and minimize. If you're looking for some middle management, panties with a reinforced front panel give extra attention to the tummy and midriff. Great under straight skirts, knits, and flat-front pants.

Control Thongs

Newer styles with a specific waist-cinching feature come in varying lengths. Some begin just under the ribs, some under the bust line, some at the waist, and compress the midsection from that point to the hips, eliminating lines at the waist and providing a smooth silhouette on the sides.

Control Shorts

Bike short styles slim from the waist to the upper leg, instantly reshaping bulging hips and thighs; they also often have a woven built-in lift feature for droopy bottoms.

◀ Control Camisole

Resembling a tight camisole or tank top, it gives a seamless, contoured look under sheer or formfitting tops that show the slightest detail of an undergarment. An often overlooked solution for those sensitive to underwire bras, or those concerned about back fat squeezed over the lat muscles by bra bands.

Bandeau-Style Full Slip ▶

Often made with a built-in underwire or molded bra that offers light support and the option of going braless, this garment offers a light compression that smoothes and firms from midriff to thigh. Sometimes available in a strapless form that looks like a tube and slims from the bust to the knee. (*And* it's great under strapless dresses.)

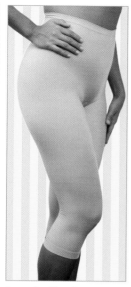

Long-leg Panties or Pants Liners

Longer leg styles create a smooth line from waist to knee (or even ankle!), offering the look of an all-over tight, toned body in a jiffy. Instant gratification.

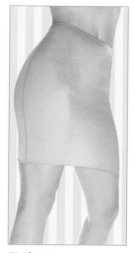

Half-slip

A shaping slip that starts at the waist and is perfect under sheer, clingy fabrics and pencil skirts; it smoothes and firms the rear, stomach, and thighs.

Body Briefer

Looks like a one-piece bathing suit. Usually made of spandex power-net, it has a built-in bra and tummy control all in one. Perfect for whittling the waist and battling a bulging belly.

◀ Strapless

Slims and smoothes the torso under fitted strapless garments, leaving the shoulders bare.

Waist-cincher/ Waspie/French Cinch

A short garment that begins at the ribs and ends above the hips. When tightened, it cinches the waist, à la Scarlett O'Hara. Made from all manner of fabrics—lace to leather—with lace-up, snap, or hook-and-eye closures, they are typically reinforced by vertical boning or stays to provide shaping. Many of today's innovative control garments have cleverly included this waist-cinching feature by weaving it into the fabric. A note: Marcel Rochas designed a version in 1947 called a *guepière* (prounounced geh-pih-yair). Nowadays, most European manufacturers use that term to describe underwire bustiers and corsets. It should not be confused with *guipure* (pronounced ghee-poor), a type of lace used in some lingerie.

WHAT TO WEAR UNDER THERE

Outside: Slinky, body-skimming gown or dress

Inside: Control panties

Just as you wouldn't wear your gym socks with heels, don't try to stuff a pair of regular panties under a special-occasion dress. Unless you want to go commando and not wear anything at all, choose your panty based on your body type. If you're worried about lumps and bumps, try laser-cut panties, which simply end seamlessly—the fabric lies flat against your body for a smooth silhouette. If you would like a little control, try a long-line or a panty that falls lower on the thigh than normal pairs. These bike short—like styles slim and support; try a pair that rests high above the waist for a totally smooth silhouette. (Some styles come right up to the bustline.) Another option is a classic pair of control-top pantyhose to keep everything nice and snug.

wrong

right

CONTROL FREAK

Q. I need more control in my shapewear. Should I go down a size?

A. Before you downsize, first try a higher control level. If you're still not satisfied, by all means *try* a smaller size. But if you're wearing anything that is so tight it causes a loss of circulation, I highly doubt you'll end up smiling, even if you manage to squeeze into some fabulously tight outfit. Believe me, a few centimeters of skin are a lot less noticeable to an onlooker than someone who looks like she is suffering.

THIGH MASTER

Q. What can I do to stop my thighs from jiggling and shaking?

A. A control brief will easily solve this problem. There are several lengths available, depending on the amount of control you want and how much area you want to cover. Choose from mini short, bike short, above-the-knee, or waist-to-ankle length and enjoy totally toned thighs under that slinky black dress or those jersey pants.

FAT GIRL SLIM

Q. I'm what I call a "skinny fat person"— although I'm thin, I don't feel toned. No matter how much I exercise, I can't get rid of my cellulite and flab. Is there a way to hide the cottage cheese so I look better in clothes?

A. A pair of shaping bike shorts, or even control-top pantyhose, will give you the smooth look you want. Since size isn't the issue as much as lumps or loose flesh, a lighter form of support should do the trick to give you toning without any cinching.

Show Some Leg

🌹 Stockings & Pantyhose & Tights, Oh My! 🌹

*U*nless you live in a place that is warm year-round, winter means piling on the clothing for months on end. In the midst of the long, drab months, stockings, pantyhose, tights, thigh-highs, and stay-ups let your legs step out into the spotlight, providing a break in all that monotonous bundling. They trace a form somewhere underneath the layers. They allow a respite from wearing pants every day. They flash a little color. They show some leg.

In the movies, the image of a woman rolling her nylon stockings on or off has always been a symbol of seduction. Though the reality of hopping around the bedroom trying to pull on a pair of tights doesn't hold quite the same allure, pantyhose *are* blessed by being both pretty and practical.

Unlike a pair of spiky high heels, they look—and feel—good.

Women often have a set notion about what kind of hosiery they will wear. Some don't consider themselves the tights type but swear by pantyhose. Some have drawers full of opaque tights in all colors and textures, and renounce sheer pantyhose as uncool. For others, it's bare-legged or bust, as anyone knows who is up on fashion magazines or has studied in the school of *Sex and the City.* Still others avoid all forms of hosiery because they find it altogether constrictive and annoying. And then what about the women who won't think beyond the blacks

Back in black: tights for the leg-lengthening look.

and nudes? Get out of your rut—with such a variety available, everyone can find something new to try.

Leg Lessons

I'm no William Safire, but if you asked me what I mean when I say hosiery, stockings, pantyhose, and tights, here's what I'd come up with:

- **Hosiery**—knitted apparel that covers the foot and/or leg, including socks, knee-highs, thigh-highs, stay-ups, stockings, pantyhose, and tights
- **Stockings**—hosiery you wear with a garter belt
- **Pantyhose**—sheer waist-to-toe fitted leg wear, often woven out of nylon or microfiber
- **Tights**—leg wear constructed like pantyhose but made from heavier, opaque, printed, or woven patterns and fabrics

To Bare or Not to Bare

*W*hether and when a woman wears pantyhose is often a matter of career, age, occasion, or season. A mother might advise her twenty-something daughter to wear pantyhose in order to appear professional on any type of job interview, while the daughter will argue back that she'll look uncool if she's trying to break into a more relaxed or style-driven field like fashion. Bottom line: Women who work in business, law, or other industries with conservative dress requirements almost always wear hosiery if they are not wearing pants. (There are also occasions, such as funerals or religious services, that call for pantyhose; bare skin is simply inappropriate.)

Whether and when a woman wears pantyhose is often a matter of career, age, occasion, or season.

Still, you can't avoid the "coolness" debate whenever you talk about tights vs. pantyhose vs. bare legs. Many young women would sooner freeze than be seen in a pair of pantyhose or tights. It's one thing to see bare legs in the same fashion spread as wool coats and fur hats in a magazine, and quite another to try that stunt on the street. It certainly makes me wonder—someone who bares her legs when it's snowing walks the line between fashion victim and frostbite victim.

At the other extreme are the women who think they're too old to get away with bare legs. They continue to wear nude pantyhose, as they always have. It serves as "makeup" for their legs, evening skin tone and smoothing the texture of the skin. Fine. But how about a little experimentation?

When dressing up for a night out, let's not forget the sex appeal, allure, and slenderizing effect of ultrasheer black hosiery under that little black dress. **Or what about a pair of tights with an intricate crochet pattern? Transforming!** Then there are pinstripe patterns, which elongate and give subtle texture. And it is possible to work in bright colors without looking like you're six years old or getting dressed for Halloween. Vivid, matte red tights, for example, when matched with a pair of

ON THE JOB

Q. I like the look of bare legs, but my office dress code requires pantyhose. What can I wear that will give a convincingly bare look but won't get me fired?

A. Good news! Some ultrasheer styles are virtually invisible on the leg. Bad news: You may have to pay a little more for a perfect match, since less expensive brands are often limited in their texture and color selection. To achieve the nude look, always choose an ultrasheer tone that is an exact match to your natural skin tone. Never go lighter, and never, ever wear cream or white stockings—the lighter the color, the larger the legs appear. (Also, the little-girl-in-her-Easter-best look doesn't work so well for grown women.)

classic boots, add pop to a simple outfit. Personally, I love tights in really rich colors like burgundy, purple, and teal. They look great with boots and pumps and can even be worn with peep-toe shoes all winter long. It used to be a faux pas to have tights sticking out of

Ultrasheer hose for the office won't offend your fashion sense.

open-toe shoes, but as long as you make sure the toe seam is tucked a little below your toes and not bunching out, you're good to go. To avoid looking too wacky or eccentric, you can pair colorful tights with shoes in the same color family for a bold, yet chic, monochromatic look.

TIGHT(S) SPOT

Q. **I like the look of tights, but they always feel so uncomfortable. They either cinch my waist, or my legs feel bound by the crotch portion. Then, if they're patterned, my bottom itches after I wear them for a while. Can I ever wear a skirt once the weather gets cold?**

A. Don't give up! Some low-quality textured woven patterns do make the wrong kind of impression—they dig in and cause itching, even if you're just sitting down. But newer styles made of lighter fibers are so unrestrictive you'll forget you're wearing them. New technologies allow for knit pantyhose to adapt not only to the shape of the leg, but also to your waist, hips, and feet. They are made of superfine, low-density fibers, and fitted with comfort waistbands, tailored gussets, and flat toe seams that are imperceptible in shoes. But even when wearing these higher quality tights, be sure you're wearing the right undies. A pair of panties with a full bum-protecting back may be more comfortable than a thong—a soft, flat surface is gentlest on the skin.

lap of luxury

High-end manufacturers have excelled in hosiery innovation—combining the sheerest, lightest fibers that really look as if you're wearing nothing at all with the best-fitting pantyhose on the planet. Such luxurious hosiery may be outside some women's budgets—and any item that can be destroyed by a hangnail cannot be considered an "investment piece."

Wear the fine print.

Still, the comfort, designs, and fit justify the indulgence. For an extra-special occasion, you really should splurge on some luxurious leg wear—especially if you have trouble finding hosiery that fits. Many women are frustrated to discover that their body measurements don't fall into the fit range on the size charts of most pantyhose packages. Better-made brands take into account variables such as waist, hips, and length of rise from crotch to waist, in addition to the usual height and weight. Consequently, wearing them is like the difference between driving a Volkswagen Beetle and a Rolls-Royce.

Wolford, for example, takes hosiery to a whole new level. They design waistband-free pantyhose that magically maintain their shape. Another style features extra fabric in the back to allow for fullness in the rear. There are even pantyhose designed with optimum pressure distribution through the leg and foot to aid in circulation. They use a wide range of fibers—something for every climate. Beyond function, it's also fun. With the incredible variety of colors, textures, and styles available nowadays, possessing every style of leg wear would be like owning an arts and crafts collection for your legs, with an infinite number of creative possibilities.

Fishing for Compliments

ashionistas who have long since sworn off pantyhose still make exceptions for fishnets. Like denim or the color black, they are never out of style. Women who usually prefer skirts with bare legs can enjoy the same level of sexiness in fishnets, since they reveal as much as they conceal. Whether knee-high, thigh-high, or pantyhose style, fishnets are very femme fatale—they're lingerie for the legs.

One of the most ideal times to wear fishnets, in my opinion, is when you feel less than ideal. For instance, even if you're hungover, exhausted, unshowered, late for work, *and* hosting a throbbing pimple on your face, I'll bet you'll still get a compliment, or at least a glance, if you're flashing the fishnets. Seriously, they have an amazing ability to overshadow the negative with their intrinsic wow-ness. Sophisticated and seriously sexy, they also, very practically, offer a little leg coverage year-round, and particularly during the dead of winter

Liz Taylor in classic fishnets.

(when tans fade and skin flakes). Any little bit helps in battling the cold, especially if you're planning on wearing open-toed shoes.

And, as if they needed any more ovation, fishnets are appropriate for women of all body types and ages. No matter what size you are, there's no reason why you can't pull off a pair of fishies! They are also not one of those

cold feet

rebecca's tip

Unless you're getting whisked directly from limo to lobby, sometimes it's just too cold to expose your skin to the elements. Buy a pair of nude pantyhose that match your skin tone and layer them under fishnets. Nobody will know it's not bare leg underneath—and if you come down with a cold, no one can blame it on improper dressing. Believe me, it's a great trick, though not a new one. (When fishnets first became popular in the mid-1800s, they were worn over nude hose.) For a bolder look, layer fishnets over a colored pair of pantyhose or tights. Cherry red or bright turquoise fabric peaking out from the crisscrossing black is a striking combination, particularly in the middle of winter. It's not necessarily something for every day, but it's fun to play around with from time to time.

TAKING THE "HO" OUT OF HOSE

Q. **How do I wear fishnets without looking like a call girl or Cyndi Lauper circa "Girls Just Want to Have Fun"?**

A. The idea is to look more like a lady than a tramp. Don't wear fishnets with an ultrashort skirt and high heels. It's too overt. Instead, pair them with a skirt that comes just above the knee to sex-up your look without sending your style straight to the nearest street corner. Since fishnets are racy in and of themselves, they should be your main fashion statement, not worn in competition with lots of patterns and prints. Fishnets let you wear basic, neutral clothing without looking too buttoned-up or stuffy.

youngish styles that makes a middle-age mother look like she's gone "tweenile." Try transforming an outfit by showing just a sliver of mesh between the hem of your skirt and the top of your boots. A fashion classic!

Let's not forget that fishnets come in other colors besides black. A nude or chocolate brown fishnet is a very chic look with a suit or dress. Beyond that, they also come in fire engine red, deep plum, or shimmery, sparkly hues. Fishnets of every shade may not be appropriate for a corporate environment, but they certainly won't make you look like you get paid by the hour.

GETTING IT ON: HOW TO PUT ON HOSIERY

Stockings and pantyhose are such delicate creatures. Tights are a little tougher, but you still have to handle them with care. Here are some tips to prevent their premature death. If you're careful, they might live long enough to need washing (see "It's a Wash," page 167) or storing (see "In Her Drawers," page 171)!

1. Check for hangnails, then gently grasp the stocking, pantyhose, or tights, bunching it up in your fingers until your thumbs have reached the tip of the toe.

2. Place one foot in so your toes are against the seams, adjusting so the fabric is properly positioned and not twisted.

3. Gradually nudge the hose up your leg (using the pads of your fingers—no fingernails), being careful to keep it straight as you slide it up. This is especially important for patterned or seamed hosiery.

4. Pull stockings to their full length (if you're wearing them with a garter belt, see "How to Put On a Garter Belt" on page 152). For pantyhose and tights, keep on going!

5. Once one leg is in, repeat the above steps for the other. If you find your tights

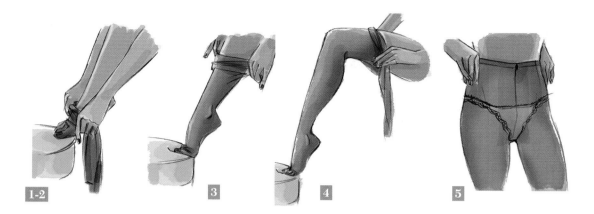

1-2 **3** **4** **5**

are coming up short, gather more material, starting at the foot or ankle. Delicately pinch both sides and work the fabric up. This is preferable to grabbing your waist with both hands and yanking up.

RUN-INS

We've all done it. You open a brand-new pair of hosiery and stick your toe right through the foot. Ruined on arrival! Or how about the way the entire world can become one big obstacle course when you're wearing a pair of special stockings that you don't want to destroy. Here are some ways to avoid a run-in with disaster:

❖ **Do a quick check of your toenails and fingernails.** Make sure there are no hangnails waiting to rip the hosiery as you pull it on. A little moisturizer can help

smooth out other rough spots on your feet that might get caught. Along with creams and lotions, keeping calluses smooth on heels and toes is another preventative. **If you need a justification to get regular pedicures, here's one:** The money you're spending might otherwise get wasted buying endless pairs of pantyhose.

❖ **Take your time.** I can't tell you how often I've put a finger through the leg or hip area because I was in a hurry. If this sounds familiar, wear gloves. Some companies even make gloves for the sole purpose of avoiding snags when putting on hosiery. I know someone who swears that storing stockings or pantyhose in the freezer before putting them on minimizes snags, but I have no proof this is true. Try it and let me know what you think!

❖ **Pay attention.** When hosiery is safely on, don't walk around barefoot. Once you're dressed, be aware of rough surfaces, especially the edges under desks and tables, that you might touch with your legs. The edges of automobile seats are notorious shredders. Even an innocent decorative purse held on your lap, or a shopping bag that bangs against your leg, can do damage. Also, be careful of the inner linings at the tops of boots and certain shoes.

SNAGGED!

It's true: Nail polish does stop snags. Coat the area with clear polish to prevent the ladder effect that occurs as a run travels. If possible, avoid putting the polish on your skin; otherwise, the stockings will stick to you. But you don't always have to bag 'em after you snag 'em. Some of my snagged stockings have enjoyed a useful second life. Sometimes I wear them as liners under pants or with long skirts and boots where they won't be seen. Admitting I've occasionally worn less-than-perfect stockings may sound inconsistent with my advocacy of beautiful lingerie at all times; however, let's be realistic. If you wear hosiery daily you'll do all you can to

make it last. Speaking of frugality, here's a trick my manager used back in the days when she wore pantyhose a lot: If she got a snag in the left leg of one pair, she'd put it aside until she snagged the right leg of another of the same style and color. She would then cut off the damaged legs of each and wear both pairs together. Two wrongs *can* make a right!

STOCKINGS & GARTER BELTS

I remember wearing stockings and garter belts at age twelve, because pantyhose weren't commonly available yet. Today, however, stockings and garters are inextricably linked with seduction. That's because of their history. Until the middle of the 1940s, when hosiery became a regular everyday item, a glimpse of stocking had been shocking. Stockings and garters went unseen. Now, because few women wear them, their image has returned to those pre—World War II erotic roots. When a woman chooses to wear stockings and garters instead of pantyhose, she is either very traditional or, more likely, making a conscious decision to go the sexier route. It's power dressing for the bedroom, and she's sending a message that even the most eyes-glued-to-the-television, butt-glued-to-the-seat guy can understand. For more on garter belts (including how the heck you wear them) see "How to Put On a Garter Belt" on page 152. While pantyhose are infinitely more practical, kittenishly seductive stockings are undeniably attractive and flirty.

Living the Thigh Life: Behold the Beauty of Stay-ups

*A*s sexy as stockings, as simple as tights, stay-ups exude all the allure of their more complicated cousin, the stocking, but don't require a garter belt or suspenders. Revealing the upper portion of the thigh, they stay in place with an elastic top band that is lined with silicone or rubber to grip the leg.

Stay-ups are great when you want leg coverage but don't want to fuss over the whole production of garters and straps. Also, in contrast to full-coverage pantyhose, they don't add another layer to your hip and waist. Then there's the matter of maybe dressing for a date when you think somebody might be seeing what's going on under your dress afterward—they're perfect for that and certainly more seductive to peel off than a pair of pantyhose. That flash of thigh is undeniably tempting! But on a strictly practical basis, when the weather is hot, stay-ups are infinitely cooler than a full pair of tights. For that and other reasons, they are (along with stockings and a garter belt) the perfect leg wear under a wedding or evening gown. Think about all the maneuvering you must do simply to use the bathroom, what with holding and protecting the dress and trying to pull

Getting down with stay-ups.

down your pantyhose. As with any undergarment, stay-ups should be taken for a test-drive before a big event, especially your wedding day.

Here's how to ensure your pair has staying power:

1. Make sure your upper thighs are free of moisturizers and powders that might compromise the effectiveness of the silicone.

2. As with a pair of stockings, gently gather the stay-up with your fingertips until you reach the toe.

3. Fold the top over so the silicone doesn't drag along your skin as you roll your stay-up over your foot and up your leg.

4. Once the stay-up is stretched to full length, flip the top over so the band is facing the right way (against your skin).

A properly positioned stay-up usually hits at about mid-thigh or higher for a comfortable, snug, secure fit. If they are too big they might not stay in place. If they are too small they can uncomfortably squeeze your leg or cause a bulging sausagelike effect.

legs, legs, legs!

It's not my intention to cover all the variations of leg wear that exist—there are simply too many—but here's the basic leggy terminology.

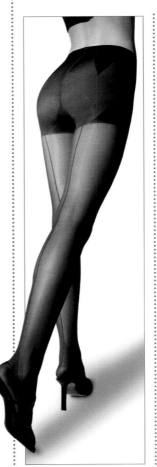

Control-top Pantyhose

As the name implies, hosiery with a panty portion containing more spandex to provide control, like a lightweight shaper. There are styles that target the tummy, while others go after the derriere and thighs. This is where hosiery and shapewear meet.

Seamed Hose

Sheer or opaque hose with a seam up the back of each leg. Before the advent of circular knitting machines, all stockings had seams up the back as a result of their construction. Later, with advances in weaving technology, the seams were no longer necessary—stockings with seams today have "mock seams," for appearance only.

Garter Belt Hose

Stockings, attached to two elastic strips that in turn connect to an elastic band around the waist. This more modern one-piece version has stockings and garter belt both built into a single garment (without any hardware).

Patterned Hose

Hosiery with designs woven in; usually made on a jacquard knitting machine, which has a versatile pattern-making mechanism. Some popular patterns are lace, herringbone, argyle, or point d'esprit.

Thigh-highs/Stay-ups

Thigh-highs include any over-the-knee hosiery. Stay-ups or hold-ups are stockings that stay up without the aid of garters. A rubber or silicone band is applied to the inner edges of the stocking tops to grip the skin around the thigh (like the inside edges of strapless bras).

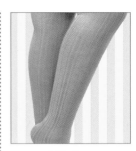

Textured Hosiery

Any style of hosiery patterned with thick and thin sections: ribbed with vertical wales, cable-knit patterns, dimensional lace, fishnet, or windowpane.

Reinforced Toe

The toe area on a stocking foot that is more densely woven to prevent toe-through. Wear the reinforced-toe style only with closed-toed shoes; otherwise, you'll look like you wandered out of a nursing home.

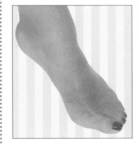

Sandalfoot Hose

Sheer hose with no visible reinforcements at the toes or heals—ideal for wear with open-toed shoes or sandals. But be gentle when pulling it over your foot!

Sheer to Waist

Sheer tights with a consistent appearance from waist to toe, ideal for a more uniform look. They lack the heavier, reinforced panty portion that is knit into many styles, with the higher risk of poking your fingers through the upper region as you pull them on. Avoid that final yank!

hot dates for hosiery

1920s ▲

☆ Art of Seduction

Originally made of silk or wool, stockings are revolutionized by new, emerging technology. Rayon, known as art (for "artificial") silk, appears in fleshlike colors that become even more sheer as time goes on.

Jane Russell tips her hat to the long, leggy look . . .

1940 ▼

☆ Hosiery Hysteria

The first nylons go on sale on May 15, 1940. More than 780,000 pairs are sold in the United States on the first day, about 40 million pairs in the first four days, and 64 million pairs in the first year. Some suggest the first part of the word *nylon* stands for New York, where the innovative fiber was introduced by DuPont at the 1939 World's Fair.

1940s

☆ Stocking Up

The country enters World War II, and nylon production is strictly devoted to the war effort. That's when women get creative, rubbing makeup or coffee on their legs to look like stockings, and using eyebrow pencils to draw lines up the backs of their legs to replicate seams. (Real nylon hosiery is strictly a black-market item.) On the first day nylons are available after the war ends, Macy's sells out its entire stock of 50,000 pairs in six hours.

1950s

☆ To Dye For

Improved dyeing techniques bring brighter, more vivid colors. And the development of spandex in 1959 eliminates that unattractive saggy, elephant-skin bunching and wrinkling around the knees and ankles.

1960s to 1970s

☆ Seamy Details

Once upon what seems a long time ago, an individual stocking was made of a single piece of fabric that was flat-knit and sewn together, creating a seam up the back of the leg. They were called "full-fashioned hose" because nylon didn't stretch, meaning that the stockings had to be "fashioned" in the shape of the leg. Beginning in the early 1960s, circular knitting machines, which can create a tube shape, make it possible for hose to fit better without the seam and with more stretchiness. By the end of the decade, very few seamed hose are made. Seams come back as a fashion statement in the 1970s, but the stockings are made by the "circular knit" method with an illusory seam knit up the back. In the hosiery biz, this is called a "mock seam."

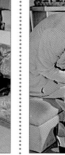

sorts of skirts, a staple in the uniform of the new corporate woman. Tights are worn with leotards and leg warmers for dancing and exercising, making way for leggings and footless tights, the decade's quintessential fashion items. Aerobicizers and punk rockers agree on one thing: spandex, worn alone or layered, in black or bright neon, stripes or lace. Twenty years later, this leggy look gets back to the future, with all forms of footless leg wear on catwalks and sidewalks.

removal and other skin treatments are on the rise—every last body hair is waxed or lasered away and skin is fake-baked or self-tanned with sunless tanners that actually leave you looking tan, not orange. Britney Spears wears her not-that-innocent combination of ultrashort skirts without any leg wear or, even racier, with just a garter on her wedding day. And Paris Hilton infamously dances on tables at clubs with absolutely nothing on underneath. Nothing.

1960s ▲

✿ Skirting the Issue

Women are wearing pantyhose of all patterns, colors, and textures, particularly fishnets and geometric square "windowpane tights." But we can't talk about tights without mentioning the international fashion icon, the mother of the mini, Mary Quant, who is said to have invented tights, or opaque

pantyhose. But the designer Cristobal Balenciaga is also credited with first introducing colorful and patterned leg wear into his collections. Quant's version, introduced in 1965, gets off to a running start, since it's the perfect thing to wear underneath her miniskirts, which are too short to be worn with traditional stockings and garter belts or girdles. In the decades since, the sales of opaque tights have always directly correlated with the relative popularity of short skirts—they are a classic coupling!

1970s to early 1980s

✿ Flashdancing & Power Dressing

Through the excessive '80s, pantyhose are worn under all

1990s to 2000s ▼

✿ Dare to Bare

The bare-leg look takes over. Simultaneously, body hair

. . . and Marilyn Monroe agrees.

Through Thick & Thin

As we've learned, hosiery can range from translucent and fine to opaque and bulky. A lot depends on the fiber content, but the other key element is the weight and thickness of the yarn, which is called *denier*—the international system for the measurement of textiles. It is used for all types of clothing, but most people come across the term when shopping for hosiery. Basically, a low denier represents finer yarns, while a higher denier indicates a heavier yarn.

Typically, the lower the denier, the more sheer the hosiery. The higher the denier, the more opaque. However, you can't base everything on denier alone. Technological advances have made it possible for hosiery to look incredibly sheer yet retain a high enough denier so the item is not as fragile. Sheer, yet strong.

Opaque (approximately 40 denier and up): You're totally covered. You will not be able to see your skin through the weave, except maybe just barely when you look at your bended knee. The high denier means a greater saturation of color as well as durability, making opaque hosiery great for everyday use. These are the tights to wear in cooler weather because they provide some warmth.

Semi-opaque (approximately 30 to 40 denier): The middle ground between opaque and sheer. You'll be able to see your skin through the weave, but it's stronger and more resilient than sheer. Also called "day sheer" or "business sheer," this weave is durable enough for long hours at the office, yet dressy enough for night.

Sheer (approximately 15 to 30 denier): The classic. Rather than concealing your legs, sheer hosiery evens out their appearance. Similar to ultrasheer, the fabric is stronger and more run- and snag-resistant. Perfect for daily wear—morning, noon, and night.

Ultrasheer (approximately 15 denier or less): When you want to look like you're wearing nothing at all . . . With the lowest denier, these stockings will keep you coolest in hot weather. Light in color and extremely delicate, nude ultrasheer hosiery is virtually translucent. This "evening sheer" is extraordinary for night and exquisite for day, though it is fragile and runs the risk of snagging easily.

FINISHING UP

Think how dramatically different a black shoe looks in regular leather and patent leather. That will give you an inkling of the different looks created by wearing hosiery with different levels of shine, which is called the finish.

Matte: A flat finish without any reflective shine. What it lacks in shininess, it often makes up for in deep, vivid, and bold colors. The effect is to downplay the legs—making this the best finish for women with large legs—while sending out a message of subdued glamour.

Slight Sheen: With about the same degree of shine as just-moisturized legs, it casts a soft light that gently highlights and contours. The natural level of shine is so flattering in sheers and nudes that, like a facial highlighter, it attracts the eye in subtle and unexpected ways. Elegant and appropriate for day, yet dressy enough for evening.

Shiny: Smooth and sleek, glam-a-rama leg wear. More glossy than glitzy, it's not as showy as sparkly or glittery hosiery. But its high, light-reflecting shine literally turns the spotlight on you. The sleek look is perfect for special occasions, and most flattering on leaner legs.

She's Got Legs!

When I see someone wearing tights or pantyhose in a particularly striking and stylish way, it reminds me of the astounding number of leg wear fashion options. Stockings, pantyhose, tights—they're like chocolate. You have your basics that you can pick up at any drugstore for a quick fix, but once you taste some of the more luxurious varieties out there, it opens a whole new world of appreciation. Hosiery, in all its forms, colors, textures, and styles, can single-handedly revive outfits long since relegated to the back of the closet. That boring old skirt you were never really into wearing can be magically transformed once it becomes the backdrop for some great leg wear. A simple dress can be dressed up. You can be casual and comfortable (and maybe not even feeling your best), but if you walk out in the right tights, pantyhose, or killer pair of fishnets, heads are going to turn. Now, that's a transformation!

Dressing to Undress

🌹 Tips for Women (and for Men) 🌹

Every layer I put on my body is significant, from the skirts, pants, blouses, and coats seen by the world, to the underwear viewed only by those to whom I grant exclusive access. It should be clear to you by now that I do not believe lingerie requires an audience to be enjoyed—I wear beautiful things when I'm alone in my beach house in the middle of winter just because it makes me feel good.

> **According to the gospel of lingerie, by wearing things that make you feel desirable, you become desirable.**

However, it's always inspiring to have someone I can take pleasure in dressing and undressing for. But while few can deny lingerie's effect on men, some women need convincing that lingerie is for their own benefit too. According to the gospel of lingerie, by wearing things that make you feel desirable, you become desirable. It's a major ego boost for you . . . and can work wonders for a relationship. It can light or—just as important— reignite the spark. A true coquette understands lingerie is just one part of her art of seduction.

Ladies' Night

There are so many things that can make us feel better—attitude, exercise, diet . . . and also good sex. Not just regular sex—good sex. When a woman has positive sexual relations, she feels great and radiates a sense of confidence and well-being that influences the people and atmosphere around her. If wearing lingerie plays any part in achieving that end, then I am all for it. Which is why I live by the philosophy of *dressing to undress*.

> More important than the look of the garments is wearing something that puts you in the mood. Because, believe me, enthusiasm is contagious.

Think of lingerie as the topping on a dessert. **It is not the substance, not the person, the relationship, or the sex itself,** but the whipped cream, the delicious extra bonus that makes it special. A man may never ask you to wear lingerie, but I can guarantee he'll be thrilled if you do. No one likes to ask for flowers, but it's always nice to get some. Like flowers, lingerie is a romantic gift that can help you feel adored and lucky in the love department. Unlike flowers, lingerie is a treat you'll both appreciate . . . and it lasts longer too!

Let me tell you, when it comes to men who know the difference between a teddy and a camisole, the consensus is this:

Lingerie is hot. But men unfamiliar with lingerie's charms may say they can take it or leave it. What's the point, they ask, when they're perfectly happy with nakedness? That's like saying what's the point of foreplay when you can just get right to it! Lingerie builds the excitement level, ever so gradually. More important than the look of the garments is wearing something that puts you in the mood. Because, believe me, enthusiasm is contagious. If a guy says he's not into lingerie, try sashaying around in a racy reveal-all number, a little peek-a-boo teaser of a chemise, or a slinky kimono. I bet he'll be into lingerie, and you, soon!

LINGERIE FOR LIFE, NOT A LIFELINE

*S*o many women use lingerie as a last-ditch effort to attract a spouse who is long gone, but that's like thinking a salad is going to compensate for a lifetime of poor diet. You can forget about it. Lingerie can increase relationship longevity by making everything a little hotter, providing novelty and fueling attraction. There's no denying it helps. But it cannot save a relationship that is already dead. It can, however, resuscitate one that still has some flicker of life left.

Before a relationship gets to a point of desperation, do things that remind you of why you love this person in the first place. Many couples get so caught up in the routines of coupledom that they forget to have fun. It's the easiest things that become the hardest. Why not make love on the kitchen floor? Live it up a little! Don't suffer from too little lingerie, too late . . . start now!

---

rebecca's tip ▶ **variety!**

Spending your love life with one person can sometimes be challenging. Variety in your lingerie wardrobe will inspire new scenarios and fantasies to stir up desire after the initial lust of a relationship starts to fade. One of the key benefits of lingerie is its ability to let you reinvent yourself. When women buy lingerie they are usually thinking only about their physical appearance—how to boost this or show that—but lingerie's power to transform from the inside is what often makes all the difference.

IF THESE WALLS COULD TALK, PART I!

Reasons Women Buy Lingerie

Over the years, women have shared with me many reasons for their lingerie purchases. The intimate boudoir setting at my store, the giddiness of all the silk and lace, and the slumber party atmosphere make people drop their drawers, so to speak, discussing topics not ordinarily shared between strangers.

Relationships are a major motivator for lingerie purchases, whether it's a love connection they're making, breaking . . . or even faking. Listen to some of what I've heard:

❀ **First date:** "Finally someone to see my sexy underwear!"

❀ **Falling in love:** "I feel good. I look good. And I want to make our first encounter really special. . . . Okay, so maybe it's our second encounter."

❀ **Getting married:** "I want the perfect underwear, under the perfect dress, on my perfect day."

❀ **Honeymoon:** "I am *not* going to be one of those wives who gives up after she ties the knot. I need things for the nuptial night . . . and every night after."

- ❦ **Anniversary:** "I can't believe we've been together for ten years. Time to start fanning the flame of passion!"

- ❦ **Marriage saver:** "I've done just about everything to get him to notice me. I'm giving it one last try."

- ❦ **Getting divorced:** "I am going to buy everything I can get my hands on before the credit cards are canceled."

- ❦ **Having an affair:** "My husband just left for London and I'm on my way to meet my personal trainer . . . but not at the gym."

LINGERING ISSUES: WHAT'S HOLDING YOU BACK?

"I don't have the body for lingerie." One of the biggest, and least justifiable, excuses for bypassing lingerie comes from women who do not want their bodies to be noticed. Making love in the dark, when your lover can't see you at all, isn't the best recipe for a fulfilling sex life, and yet it's hard for a lot of women to feel comfortable cavorting in the nude. And that is exactly why lingerie makes so much sense. It lets you highlight what you want to display and hide what you want to downplay. I've heard men jokingly call push-up bras "false advertising," but you know what?—at least it got their attention! When you wear beautiful lingerie, you are serving yourself on a silver platter, complete with garnishes. It masks some of your insecurities, and you'll come off exuding the confidence of a courtesan. It's impossible to attain full intimacy with someone you keep at arm's length. And that, my dear, is why there is intimate apparel!

"Lingerie isn't really my style." With such a diverse range available, saying "Lingerie isn't *me*" means nothing. When a woman tells me this, I take her by the arm and show her safer, subtler types of lingerie until she stops saying "Me? In that?" and admits that she might actually wear some of what I've shown her. My diagnosis is that protesting women really mean one of two things: 1) "I wouldn't wear a cutout lace teddy," or 2) "I don't know how he's going to react to seeing me in something like that." The first concern is no problem, since there are plenty of subdued styles that are still seriously suggestive. All a woman has to do is pick out something that pleases her, that makes her feel beautiful and relaxed. The rest will follow. One of my customers put it this way, "After I bought new silk pajamas, let's just say that my husband told me—and showed me—that he didn't need Viagra anymore."

The second concern is, in the end, really mostly about bravery. If you've never brought lingerie into the picture, it's not so easy revealing that more adventurous part of yourself to someone unless there is real trust. While you might secretly hope to be a seductress, it's another thing to face your lover and have the response be, "Um, what are you doing?" I advise men who are buying lingerie for the first time to start slowly with tamer items and work their way up to the more exotic and erotic; the same applies to women.

Lingerie is meant to be worn *your* way. You don't have to assume a different persona (unless you want to). It's perfectly okay to giggle and blush. You might even feel more comfortable joking around a little, acknowledging the humor in the situation by jumping out and saying "Ta da!" Since your experience will most likely not be a perfectly orchestrated lovemaking scene from a movie, embrace the reality of limbs falling asleep, the occasional "oops," and "sorry about that"—it doesn't have to be so serious. Stop thinking of Lingerie with a capital *L*.

"A woman undressing is like the sun emerging through the clouds."
—AUGUSTE RODIN

IF THESE WALLS COULD TALK, PART II!
More Reasons Women Buy Lingerie

Body-related issues often provide another impetus for intimates:

❁ **Weight loss:** "I deserve a reward—and I don't mean chocolate."

❁ **Makeover:** "I'm tired of the old me. Time for a change. What should I buy?"

❁ **After-the-baby boost:** "Now it's time for me. That nursing bra is toast! My boobs are mine again."

❁ **New boobs:** "At last I can wear all those beautiful bras I've always been jealous of and wanted to wear."

It's All About the Packaging

Lots of men lust for lingerie. Most go for black—that's the number one color. They also love sheerness. Black *and* sheer? It's a lethal combination that will drive him crazy. Some men, however, like revealing mesh and lace, while others prefer opaque. Some get excited by the white cotton, girl-next-door, cheerleader rah-rah look, and others want the lustful vamp, complete with garter belt and stockings.

> **Your lover should feel the anticipation as you slowly peel away the layers of clothing . . . and any emotional distance.**

For the time being, forget about what he wants. You are not a statue that can be unveiled with a flick of the wrist. You are a complicated woman who wants a lover to feel the anticipation as you slowly peel away the layers of clothing . . . and any emotional distance. And on any given night, you may feel like revealing different sides of your personality. That's why my advice is to mix things up! *That* is exhilarating.

I'm in the lingerie business, so it's easy for me to say, but I really believe you can never have too much lingerie. At the very least, go through items on this page and vow to try a little something. And then try something else.

boudoir basics

Every coquette needs at least one of each of the following:

A pretty robe

When you're not ready to reveal it all, a silky robe suggests the promise of a slow, simmering seduction, one layer at a time.

A long gown

Long, lean, and luxurious, the key to being seductive without showing too much. A gown makes a woman feel glamorous . . . and a lover curious about what is underneath.

A bra & panty set

When you peel off your clothing nothing impresses more than a matching ensemble. Name your style. Name your color. Let him meet his match.

Black & sheer

No lingerie drawer is complete without something, anything, in this dynamic duo. And when there's a little lace too . . . look out!

A half-time outfit

Somewhere between nakedness and clothing, this kind of outfit—maybe a babydoll, or a camisole with matching shorts—can dizzy even the most diehard jock (or computer geek) to distraction. Touchdown!

A thong ▶

Don't worry about your derriere, he'll keep his eyes on the thong itself— after all, it is the idea of the thong that arouses interest. Small in size, big in rewards, a thong spells enticement.

A garter belt ▶

Purely erotic, conjuring up carnal pleasure and naughtiness.

Bridal Sweet

An upcoming wedding is often the first time a woman feels comfortable and fully justified going on a lingerie-buying binge. That's why I love working with brides-to-be—they're so open and eager to start this new phase of their lives. They're crossing a major threshold, and they not only need to figure out what to wear under the dress (see page 63), but they want to stock up on everyday basics and round out their collection with flirty items they've been looking for an excuse to buy.

WEDDING NIGHT

Oh, what to wear when your big day turns into your big night? Anything you want. A lot of brides prefer the traditional and elegant two-piece peignoir set. The long robe and flowing gown is usually in white, ivory, and pastel shades. If you've always dreamed of that fairy-tale wedding night, here's your chance—you might as well go all out. For the nontraditional, a short silky chemise or camisole and tap pant set might do the trick. For the rebel, a thong-back teddy in a bright color is the way to wow.

for honeymooners

Day 1 Virginal

Signature color: white. Angelic material makes even the most daring designs seem demure. Evoke the college coed in a tank undershirt with boyshorts. Oh-so-innocent ruffle-bottom bloomers or lace-trim bikinis bring out the Lolita within. Charming and modest eyelet lace is an eyeful. Panties that let just a little cheek peek out are a sweet reminder of first experiences. When you're as pure as the driven snow, things can only get a little dirtier.

"OH, HONEY"

For the honeymoon, I always suggest something different for every night. Each ensemble is intended to create a scenario that is different from the last—and make your lover wonder what's next on the menu. Having trouble understanding what I mean? Just think of those days-of-the-week panties . . . this is the grown-up version.

SEVEN DAYS, SEVEN WAYS

Day 2 **Femme fatale**

Signature color: black. The seductress dresses in the full ensemble of bra, panty, and garter belt. Animal prints and corset-style lacing reveal your wild side. Stockings, fishnets, and thigh-high stay-ups complete the seduction. If you've ever dreamed of showing up in a trench coat with nothing (or next to nothing) on underneath, here's your chance.

Day 3 **The vamp**

Signature color: red. Beware, the lady is a vamp. Bring on the bold, breast-boosting, behind-baring lingerie. Corsets and bustiers are just the beginning. Take charge of the situation with just a hint of soft and safe bondage— maybe a silky blindfold. Nothing too torturous for this madame— just pushing the envelope for a steamy, smoldering seduction between consenting adults.

for honeymooners

Day 4 **The sporty girl**

Signature colors: any. A good sport is always game for some action. Simple, streamlined shapes fit your style. Cotton and supersmooth microfibers are close fitting, and not too froufrou. Camisoles and tanks. Boyshorts and hipsters. These are classic and modern looks that are hot without being over-the-top.

Day 5 **The glamour queen**

Signature colors: jewel tones. Undress like a goddess. The richest materials make you ready for rapture—silk, satin, lace, velvet, and embroidery. Go ahead, embellish with pleats, tucks, rhinestones, sparkles, and all sorts of ornaments. Screen-siren marabou or a long evening gown are the essence of come-hither glam. Keep your jewelry on with a pearl thong (more on that later). All hail the queen!

SEVEN DAYS, SEVEN WAYS

Day 6 The old-fashioned romantic

Signature colors: pastels. Turn yourself into an irresistibly sweet and tempting confection of ruffles, ribbons, flounces, and frills. Lighten up with the softest cotton or dreamy chiffon in romantic baby pinks, sky blues, mints, peaches, and delicate florals. Girly boyshorts and camisoles trimmed with lace, pin tucks, embroideries, and bows. Who can say no to your girlish charm?

Day 7 The sex kitten

Signature colors: pink and black. This feline likes to receive—and knows how to get what she wants. Tempt desire with long satin gloves, stiletto slippers, flyaway babydolls, and anything peek-a-boo that brings out the exhibitionist within. Ruffles, frills, and over-the-top marabou puffs are perfect for a romp. Flash some sass with cheeky panties and side-tie bottoms just asking to be unlaced. A fun, flirty tease that's sure to please, you don't have to take off your clothes to have a good time. Lingerie is like catnip for the sex kitten!

Easy Access ✿ Accessories!

Accessories make the outfit—especially when they're the only thing you're wearing. While some lingerie items are not so explicit, certain accoutrements send your message loud and clear. Lust! It does take a little bit of daring—or maybe some wine—but why not try something new? These things are not for every day, just for those moments when you want to put the "access" back in accessories. Believe me, something a little out of the ordinary can make an extraordinary difference.

GET A GRIP
The Garter Belt

What is the mystique about the garter belt? Maybe it's that, for practical purposes, garter belts are obsolete; they exist only for pleasure—a symbol of sexiness from an era when an above-the-knee glimpse could still elevate a guy's pulse. One of my customers, an international call girl, has bought so many black garter belts that I had to ask her why. Her reply? "It's my clients' number one request." Why? "Because their wives won't wear them." Note to all you married women: Put on a garter belt before your husband requests it of someone else. See what happens. Personally, I love wearing a garter belt and silk stockings. I love the way it makes me feel. And I love the reaction I get.

HOW TO PUT ON A GARTER BELT

Most women have no clue how a garter belt should be placed or where the stockings go. This contraption isn't as complicated as it appears, but you never know until you try!

1. Start off naked and put the garter belt on, closing it so it rests comfortably on your hip bones. It should fit snugly enough to stay in place when it is tugged at from the bottom—it shouldn't be pulled down by the stockings.

2. Slide stockings on carefully, without twisting, as described in the step-by-step "Getting It On: How to Put On Hosiery," page 130. Once your stockings are properly positioned, grab the top of the stocking in front and hook it onto the clip that hangs straight down from the body of the garter belt.

3. Then do the same to the top of the stocking at the back of your leg.

4. Stand straight in front of a mirror and adjust the strap length of each garter as needed.

5. Now put on your thong or panties—*over* your garter belt. This allows you more . . . freedom.

DRIPPING IN JEWELS
The Pearl Thong

For a thong that finally rubs you the right way, try the infamous Bracli pearl thong. The Bracli's unfortunate, vegetable-sounding name was created by combining *braga,* the Spanish word meaning "panty," with *cli,* for "clitoris." Odd, yes, but people are apparently willing to look past the name—

this little runaway wonder flew off the shelves when I introduced it in my store.

So what has made this thong a legend? Its crotch consists of a single string of Mallorcan pearls. Invented by a Spanish gentleman for his wife, their once-private creation came up during a dinner party conversation; one of the guests suggested they sell the design in a hotel boutique. Needless to say, women seemed to enjoy it. When the man decided to market the thong in the United States, he telephoned me.

He didn't speak any English, and I didn't speak Spanish, but I got the gist of what he was saying (what can I say, the language of lingerie is universal!) and told him to send me one. Now, you know

Pearls are a girl's best friend.

by now that I'm not easily shocked, but even I was a little surprised when I took the beaded number out of the package. We carried the Bracli for about two years—selling it quietly and very, very well—before it caused a sensation (literally) when Samantha (who else?) wore it on *Sex and the City*.

The Bracli thong redefines the term *autoerotic*. It gives you hours of foreplay without anyone having to lift a finger. You may even want to leave it on during, if you know what I mean. But this is not an everyday item . . . as Samantha learned, after she walked up too many flights of stairs.

PUFF PIECE
*Marabou Slippers and
Other Necessary Accessories*

Fluffy, fabulous, and completely frivolous, classic marabou slippers are a glamorous symbol of sexiness worn by screen stars and sex kittens across the globe. Fantasy footwear takes any outfit, or lack thereof, to new heights.

And then turn your attention to creating ambience: candles, scented sachets, incense, pillows, high-thread-count sheets, rose petals, mood-setting music, champagne, and all manner of aphrodisiacs and toys. These romantic accoutrements might sound like

one big cliché, but let's not be too jaded, because . . . guess what? They work!

RECIPE FOR ROMANCE
scents and sensuality

Smell is one of the strongest memory senses. To set the stage for seduction, or just for yourself, here's an easy recipe that I whip up at home to create an instantly alluring aroma.

CLOVE POTION

1. Fill a medium-size pot with water.
2. Add a bunch of whole cloves and a few cinnamon sticks.
3. Turn the heat on medium until the water reaches a boil. Keep at a low simmer for as long as you like, refilling with more water as it evaporates. Never leave it unattended.

Note: Since the beginning of written history, cloves and cinnamon have been said to stir up desire. (Hey, "sin" + "a man" sounds sexy to me!) Another tantalizing scent is vanilla—use vanilla sachets to sweeten up the contents of your dresser drawers!

Remember to use common sense—a little scent will fill your entire home. During the fall and winter, I put together my little concoction as soon as I walk in the door. I call it my witch's brew because of its brownish color and floating twigs. It's a cost-effective way to, quite literally, spice things up. If someone does drop by, they inevitably ask about the delicious wafting scent.

Maternal Flame

No booze. No meds. No sushi? No coffee!!! Pregnancy might not be easy, but at least pregnant women are no longer viewed as the demure, frumpy matrons of yesteryear. Mothers-in-the-making are powerful, erotic, sexy symbols of femininity worthy of gracing the covers of national magazines.

> **Mothers-in-the-making are powerful, erotic, sexy symbols of femininity worthy of gracing the covers of magazines.**

Just because you can't sneak a drink and a smoke, it doesn't mean all forms of evening activities have to come to a halt. It's up to you (and maybe the estrogen surging through your body) to decide if you want to wear lingerie during pregnancy. All women like to feel appreciated, but some might not want to be seen as sexual objects. On the other hand, some pregnant women manage to have the excitement level of a sixteen-year-old boy—particularly during that glorious second trimester!

If that describes you, by all means wear anything that fits. As you get closer to showtime, you can still wear babydolls, nighties, or camisoles with empire waists. Long gowns will beautifully skim over your curves, accentuating your miraculous shape. And don't think you have to give up gracing your backside with all forms of frills for nine months. Low-rise briefs and thongs sit perfectly below most bellies. If you find that you're not in the mood for love, you can still sit pretty in a poet shirt or an embellished or embroidered tunic.

No frumpiness for your beautiful bump!

The Frill of It

Lingerie appeals to the biggest sexual organ: the brain. With its inherent playfulness, lingerie tempts, teases, and flirts its way into our minds. I often imagine, "What scenario will I create today?" and I'm always excited to see how it all plays out.

> With its inherent playfulness, lingerie tempts, teases, and flirts its way into our minds.

At my store, I like when I'm able to talk someone into trying something very risqué that she would never, ever have thought of wearing. Many women never dream of donning a pearl thong because of how highly erotic it is. But they should! And to bring out that side in a person, to then have them report back and say with a wink, "Now that was wonderful"—that makes me feel good. And I am most certain it makes them feel good too!

A famous twenty-two-year-old actress visited the store because she was having an affair with an older man. She came back and told me that the lingerie she purchased that day changed her love life—the sex was explosive. So is it the thrill of the chase? The fantasy? I say it's the mystical mix of one part lingerie and one part mind-set. Lingerie shows that you are adventurous, interested in the possibilities, and perhaps willing to try things you've never done before. Even if you are timid at first, it hints that you may be open to a pleasant surprise.

And I, for one, love surprises. It's incredible when you don't know what the guy's going to do (and when he doesn't know what you are going to wear). Maybe you just met him and you feel the fire getting very, very warm and he does something a little different from other men you've been with. Or maybe you're with someone you love deeply, or someone with whom you're simply having a wonderful time, and you give each other such pleasure. Wearing lingerie lets you acknowledge your own erotic and sexual potency. And, funny thing is, there's something old-fashioned about wearing beautiful lingerie, even given its adults-only nature. It lets you take things a little slower, allowing you to savor every moment as the experience builds like a musical crescendo. No matter how wild or mild, everyone, every once in a while, should dress to undress. So go ahead and start a love affair . . . with lingerie.

The Gentleman's Club

I get such a kick out of watching men steal furtive glances through the windows of my store as they walk back and forth, finally working up the nerve to enter. It happens all the time. I never cease to be amused, but I know how intimidating lingerie shopping can be for men when they're *with* a lady companion, let alone when they step into a store without proof that they're not browsing for themselves. I do as much as I can to make the experience for men as comfortable as possible. As seriously as we take lingerie, we know it's not that serious! Lingerie is supposed to be about the pleasure principle, and buying it should be no different. So, gentlemen, start your engines . . . because this section is geared just for you.

Treat the lady in your life with the gift of lingerie.

First of all, accept the fact that entering a lingerie store, no matter how confident you are, may be a little awkward at first. You're entering a woman's domain. It's hard to come up with an equivalent environment that a woman might find herself in. While a woman might feel temporarily lost or outnumbered in a sports bar on game night, she'll never stick out like a man in a hushed, high-end lingerie boutique. A fellow surrounded by those pastel walls, gilded mirrors, rows of perfectly spaced padded hangers suspending wisps of lace and straps with tags that bear names he'd feel like an idiot trying to pronounce—let alone even begin to know what their functions are—is a sight to behold. I am so tickled every time a guy picks up a lacy little nothing and asks, "What *is* this . . . and *how much* did you say it costs?"

Price is the next thing you should brace yourself for. In cost per square inch, lingerie is more expensive than real estate. It might seem extravagant to pay so much for things that are so small, but fabric content, craftsmanship, and country of origin are the details that count when it comes to lingerie. It's safe to assume that the lingerie she'll really appreciate will often cost more than you expect, so get ready for sticker shock—especially if you're the kind of guy who buys his boxers in a triple-pack for less than ten bucks. Are you ready? A pair of beautiful panties can cost twenty dollars . . . or upward of two hundred. But what could fall higher on the romance continuum than giving a lovely little piece of nothing?

Lingerie is in the upper echelon of personal gifts—somewhere around jewelry, but more personal. It is the gift appropriate only for a woman you get naked with. Of course, as with all forms of communication, motive plays a huge part. So, just as a letter written about love is very romantic, and a "Dear Jane" letter is cold as ice, lingerie given to get you out of the doghouse or into our pants doesn't carry the same level of intimacy as a gift given with a more loving intent.

Lingerie is something that both the giver and the getter should enjoy, so buy something that will satisfy both of you, not just your porn fantasy (at least not at first).

rebecca's TIP

Dr. Lauren Martin, one of my longtime customers and a psychologist in the neighborhood, recently told me, "A woman likes to feel like she is her man's fantasy; that he's not thinking about somebody else in lingerie, but fantasizing about her." Dr. Martin says men are often intimidated to buy lingerie for their partners, but encourages them to do so. She's seen enough cases to know that though a woman may feel secure in her role as the mother, the wife, or even the lover, she doesn't feel as convincing as the sexual fantasy.

Rebecca's Diagnosis: Too few men buy lingerie for their ladies.

Prescription for Men: Take two things (your lover and her new lingerie) before bedtime. You'll feel better in the morning!

Like foreplay, take it slowly with the lingerie and work your way up—don't start with the skimpiest, sheerest thing if she's shy or you don't know her well. She might end up feeling inadequate or resentful, and instead of having a wild night in bed, you could end up sleeping on the couch. Think of it this way: It would be as if she gave you

THE ROMANCE CONTINUUM				
Least Intimate ⟶				**Most Intimate**
Communication:	text message	e-mail	letter	phone call	in person
Gift Giving:	flowers	chocolate	perfume	jewelry	lingerie

a toupee for your balding, thinned-out hair because she always fantasized about a man with a full head of luscious locks. I doubt you'd warm to such a "gift" even if she said, "Try it. You'll feel sexier."

Get in the habit of buying lingerie early on in a relationship. It sends the message that you see the lady in your life as an object of desire. (I'm not talking about objectifying women. Personally, I like to see myself as the *objective,* rather than the *object,* in the bedroom.) I can't think of a woman who wouldn't love for her boyfriend or, more significantly, her husband of thirty years to buy her some exquisite lingerie. She may not ever ask, but I promise she'll appreciate your honest effort to buy her something you truly believe she will love. Giving lingerie shows her you think she deserves to be pampered and spoiled with luxuries befitting a queen.

SO, HERE'S WHAT TO DO . . .

First of all, the salesperson doesn't assume you're buying for yourself, so it's not necessary to insist that it's a *gift for someone else.* Trust me, you are not the first male customer to come through the door. In fact, although women purchase the majority of lingerie, it's the men who are doing the bulk of the buying around holidays such as Christmas, Mother's Day, and Valentine's Day. Salespeople who work in intimate apparel know you might be nervous, and are so passionate about their products that they are more than happy to guide you along. That's how it is in my store— we love a guy who loves lingerie! We're like doctors with this stuff—professional, confidential, and wanting to find just the right remedy. I like to think I may be personally responsible for many engagements, marriages, and even babies in the world (or at least New York City) because I steered a guy toward the right piece of lingerie.

◀ REBECCA'S TIP

laptop lingerie

There's something to be said for actually touching and feeling items that are primarily meant to be, well, touched and felt, but if you truly can't bring yourself to enter a lingerie store, another option is online shopping. You can privately browse on your computer screen, spend as much time as you need, and nobody has to know. I don't know how every website works, but ours (www.thelittleflirt.com), like our store, is very men-friendly. We have loyal male customers still shopping with us for their twenty-fifth wedding anniversary—and a few who are buying lingerie for their second or third wife! There are online tips to guide you through your purchase, and if you're still not sure, our customer service staff have helped many a man through his purchase over the phone. Luckily for the very busy—and the very embarrassed—you no longer have to show your face in a lingerie boutique to get the goods.

SIZE MATTERS

*T*he most common question you'll hear saleswomen ask male shoppers is, "What size is she?" That's because most of them come in without measurements. The guessing game is fun, but a little strategic planning is a good idea. Here are four ways to make this mission possible:

1. Do some detective work. Sneak a peek inside her drawers—her lingerie drawers! Find the type of item you are looking to buy, or something similar, and locate the size. Check out a few tags, because sizes vary from brand to brand. Beware of items at the back of the drawer that you've never seen her wear. She could be one of those ladies who hangs on to items that haven't fit for years, dreaming of the day she'll lose those last ten pounds. If you size her up based on a single item only, Murphy's Law guarantees you will choose one of those ancient relics. Do your reconnaissance work and capture the necessary information: her average size!

2. Ask her best friend. Girlfriends tend to know these kinds of things about each other. If she doesn't know, she'll probably be able to find out. A good friend will happily be an accomplice on this operation.

3. Ask her. Do this well before you plan to go shopping. While you're at it, get all of her sizes (bras, panties, clothes, shoes, even ring finger . . . and don't forget favorite colors too). There's something to be said for a man who has done a proper background check—and who carries all of his lady's sizes around in his wallet, ready at a moment's notice.

4. Take the Fruit Test. If you have not obtained her bra size, and can't track down her actual digits, here's your last resort: a visual aid to help you approximate her size. Just imagine which of these fruits most resembles her breasts in size or volume:

Plum: Is she cute and compact? She's probably a AA cup or smaller.

Lemon: Budding and beautiful? Try an A cup.

Orange: Ample and alluring? She's probably a B.

Grapefruit: Is she full and fabulous? Think C cup.

Cantaloupe: Voluptuous and va-va-voom? She's probably a D cup or even a DD.

Honeydew: Is she bodacious and bountiful? She's probably a DD cup or larger.

The Style Guide

This is where the fun begins! When you start out, it's important to recognize which styles afford more leeway in the size department. Men often automatically go for bras as presents because they house what may be a particularly favorite body part. But the sizing of bras can be tricky. Chemises, slips, nighties, and robes are more forgiving and come in everything from classic cotton to scandalously sheer lace to marabou-trimmed chiffon. Instead of asking the salesgirl, "What will be good for my wife?" come prepared to talk—about what she likes, and what she looks like.

> Men often automatically go for bras as presents because they house what may be a particularly favorite body part.

Start by eliminating anything that accentuates a part of the body she's sensitive about. If she's ever mentioned hating her thighs, stomach, breasts, bottom . . . or even her upper arm flab, take her word for it. This is not a time to try to disprove her theories.

ASSET MANAGEMENT

If she is sensitive about . . .

✿ **Hips or thighs:** Try a chemise, slip, or pajamas that flow loosely over that area.

✿ **Derriere:** Find something that doesn't hug the hips—a chemise, slip, long gown, pajamas, or camisole set with fluttery shorts. Choose fabrics that drape and don't cling.

✿ **Cellulite:** Get her something that deemphasizes her dimples; otherwise, if she's self-conscious about cellulite on her buttocks, she'll be moonwalking backward in the bedroom. Try a silky slip that hits at the knee and skims the body, or maybe a low-cut camisole or a gown with an open back that shows off the body parts she likes.

✿ **Tummy or waist:** Go for anything with an empire bodice that flaunts her top but is breezy and flowy beneath. Babydolls fit this bill.

✿ **Large breasts:** A beautiful bra in a larger size is something every big-busted girl appreciates. Also look for camisoles or nightgowns with extra support sewn into the garment. Tracking down supportive and seductive styles in larger sizes once felt like searching for the Holy Grail, but I promise you they're out there; all you have to do is ask.

✿ **Small breasts:** A demi-cup bra can make any girl on the A-list feel voluptuous. Camisoles and nighties with ruffles, ribbons, lace, and contrasting textures over the bodice create the illusion of more volume on top.

✿ **Legs:** A long gown is the answer. If she wears pajamas, upgrade her to an elegant silk pair.

✿ **Upper arms:** She might feel like she's getting the cold shoulder in anything sleeveless, so look for something with sleeves. Chemises and gowns with fluttery sleeves, robes, short silky wraps, or kimonos will arm her with confidence.

✿ **She's pregnant:** You want the soon-to-be mother of your child to feel appreciated, but with her body changing and hormones raging, it's important to tread carefully. Play it safe with loose, comfortable items that have empire waists

(fitted at the chest, loose below). Poet shirts or tunics are beautifully bohemian. Think about things that can serve as luxurious replacements for her favorite pajamas, baggy sweatpants, and old T-shirts.

certifiably gifted ⬤ rebecca's TIP

If you're really stuck on what lingerie to select, never underestimate the value of a gift certificate to a lingerie store. Not all women like men to shop for their intimate apparel. Some are difficult to fit, while others have very particular tastes. A regular at my store used to be so peeved when her boyfriend surprised her with expensive silky underthings from his travels in Italy—he kept buying her styles she didn't like and that didn't fit properly, and they couldn't be returned or exchanged. A gift certificate is a sure thing. The only thing you have to worry about is how much!

all wrapped up ⬤ rebecca's TIP

If the store where you buy the lingerie offers gift wrapping, take them up on it. We love pretty packages, pastel-colored tissue paper, and silky ribbons! Your thoughtful, carefully selected purchase will get a much better reception if it is delivered in a tempting wrapping that, like lingerie, is seductively designed to lead to the present within.

The Final Factor

COLORS AND FABRICS

The number one thing men go for in my shop is anything black and sheer. Is black and sheer sexy? You bet. But it's not the only thing. You want to consider her eye and hair color and skin tone. Also, does she like certain colors more than others? Does she go for the understated or the bold? I like colors myself—and wear every shade in the spectrum, depending on my mood. Sometimes I love virginal white, sometimes I want to be a vamp. Other times I want to act like her royal highness in jewel tones, or feel pretty in pastels. I'll say it again and again: The beauty of lingerie is in its ability to transform. Think about what she usually wears and fantasize about what might bring out another side. You should also feel the fabrics and choose something that is soft, smooth, and sensuous. Nothing rough or scratchy! Look for something you won't be able to keep your hands off.

> **The beauty of lingerie is in its ability to transform. Think about what she usually wears and fantasize about what might bring out another side.**

Happy Endings

A final note: Don't take it too hard if your carefully chosen item has to be returned. This is very common, not just with lingerie, but also with most types of clothing. Hey, you can even go with her to exchange it and pick something out together. What you have to remember is that it's you she'll be thanking for making her feel instantly gorgeous, decadent, and totally appreciated. Sure, you could take her to a fabulous dinner at a five-star restaurant. But, unlike a meal, lingerie has no calories, and its effect lasts much, much longer.

Long Live Lingerie

❧ Care and Upkeep ❧

he bra is one item you should purchase in quantity. If you've found the perfect one, and still love it after you've worn it a few times, go back and buy several. The more bras you have in rotation, the longer each one will last (and not just because you wear it less, but because all clothes need "time off"). Plus, if the style gets discontinued, you've got insurance.

> Like a good relationship, lingerie requires a little extra effort—along with proper care and attention to details—to make it last.

But don't be fooled into thinking a bra is "perfect" simply because it doesn't bind. If the band feels big in the beginning, it will become too loose too soon—especially if you don't give your bras a break. They need time to bounce back between wearings.

Think about how stretched out your jeans get between washings. Material stretches over time from wear and tear, body heat, perspiration, and any lotions and perfumes you put on your skin. If you wear the same bra day in, day out, it will lose its elasticity.

Bra-vo! Making Bras Last

So, now for the million-dollar question: How often *should* you wash your bra? Some women claim to wash their bras after each wearing. I find that very hard to believe! Unless you are extraordinarily vigilant or have a maid waiting on you hand and foot, you probably don't have the time (or inclination) to wash your bra that often. In fact, the average is usually along the lines of three to five wears per wash, and sometimes even more.

> **As a general rule of thumb, I recommend washing a bra every other time you wear it; however, don't start looking for an absolute, hard-and-fast rule.**

As a rule of thumb, I recommend washing a bra every other time you wear it; however, don't start looking for an absolute, hard-and-fast rule. A lined or cotton bra will get dirtier than a sheer lace bra and will need more frequent washing. Perspiration has a tendency to stain delicate fabrics while breaking down the spandex, so if your chest tends to perspire, you may need to wash your bra after each wear.

REBECCA'S TIP ▶ **take a bath!**

Rushed for time? Bring yesterday's lingerie into the shower with you!

Dark clothing often rubs off on light-colored bras; they'll end up looking dingier sooner if not washed more frequently. That's just one of the reasons I emphasize the importance of diversifying your bra collection—you don't want to end up wearing the same favorite white or nude bra underneath all your clothing. To delay discoloration and fight fading, wear dark or colored bras under dark or colored clothing. The same color is preferable, but black is always good because stains won't show. Remember, though, just because a black bra looks clean doesn't mean it isn't dirty. All bras need washing.

It's a Wash

You may not believe this, but some women consider doing laundry by hand therapeutic. They find it relaxing . . . a way to wash their cares away. I, however, am not one of them. But that doesn't mean I toss my lingerie into the washing machine. And if you want your bras and special lingerie to last, you won't either.

> You may not believe this, but some women consider doing laundry by hand therapeutic.

SOAP OPERA

Everyone and her sister has an opinion about what suds are best for your duds and underduds. For intimates, I highly recommend using a specially designed lingerie wash, such as La Blanc Linen Wash. A gentle, nonchlorinated detergent made for washing baby clothes will also work well. If you're traveling and in a pinch, shampoo—or, even better, baby shampoo—will do the trick. Bras, especially, respond better to the glorious soap stars I mentioned above. Also, bleach is a major no-no for your intimate apparel—it is much too harsh and will basically eat the spandex alive. Instead, treat soiled areas directly with soap, extra rubbing, and a longer soak time.

THE RULES OF WASHING

1. Wash intimate apparel in tepid to lukewarm water. Use slightly cooler water for bras, shapewear, and other highly elasticized items; the fabric actually gets "shocked" back into shape in colder water. Avoid hot water, which will break down the elastic and shrink natural fibers.

2. Soak the garments in soapy water for a few minutes. Give attention to soiled areas by gently rubbing the fabric between your fingers to remove any stains.

3. Rinse well, then gently squeeze out the water—never wring. Smooth the garment out with your hands and hang to dry away from sunlight or heat. For items that hold excess moisture (like cottons or sweater-type knits), lay the item on a towel, roll it up like sushi, and squeeze. Then reshape the garment and either hang or lay it flat to air dry.

Got Silk?

*S*ilk lingerie, such as slips and camisoles, often pose a laundry quandary. First and foremost, follow the manufacturer's instructions for care. Very often, the label calls for dry cleaning, which might make you think silk and water are enemies. Not so. Silk is actually refreshed by water. The reason manufacturers suggest dry cleaning is because interfacings (used to stiffen collars, cuffs, etc.) and linings are sometimes made from different fabrics that have different shrink rates than the silk, causing puckering if washed. But if your lingerie is pure silk, hand wash it. To get out excess moisture, squeeze gently (don't wring or twist) and then shake the item with a good, hard whipping motion. Smooth the garment out with the palms of your hands, hang it up, and air dry. To remove any wrinkles, use a warm-to-hot iron on the inside of the garment while it is still damp.

> **Very often, the label calls for dry cleaning, which might make you think silk and water are enemies. Not so. Silk is actually refreshed by water.**

Personally, I always prefer hand washing intimate apparel to dry cleaning. The solvents and heat are hard on fabrics, smell bad, and as far as I'm concerned, aren't truly effective at cleaning. Not to mention the potentially hazardous chemical compounds—it's one thing to have them on your winter coat, but quite another when they are touching your most delicate areas.

Silk is sensuous, and easy to care for.

silk saver   ▶ REBECCA'S TIP

If you accidentally get water stains on 100 percent silk, don't get distraught. Washing the entire garment will get rid of the marks.

Rage Against the Machine

Your delicate items don't stand much of a chance against the rough agitation of the washing machine. (Most hosiery is so delicate that some pantyhose and stockings don't even last long enough to warrant washing.) The fabric may tangle up and bunch, while underwires in bras may bend, lose their shape, pop out, or get caught in the machine itself. If you absolutely must machine wash, first hook your bras closed and then put all like items in a mesh lingerie bag (a protective net bag with a nylon zipper closure). Use tepid water on the delicate cycle with a gentle or lingerie detergent. Never throw lingerie in with heavy or heavily soiled things like jeans and towels—these bulky items will beat the living daylights out of your lingerie!

HIGH & DRY

In the end, there's only one major rule for lingerie laundering: always air dry. The heat from the dryer is far too intense and will cause elastic to break down or melt and the garment to lose its shape and fit. Cotton and wool will become miniatures of their former selves, and elasticity will be *g-o-n-e* from any control garments. It may feel like a movie cliché, racing into the bathroom to gather up damp undergarments before an unexpected guest sees them. But why not flaunt it? Many women's fashion magazines actually recommend strewing your skimpiest little somethings in the shower for special guests to notice. My store manager, Barbara, likes the way they look hanging in her bathroom, like delicate flags of femininity waving a promise of something delightful and naughty to the person who happens upon them.

lingerie life span

REBECCA'S TIP

Believe it or not, many lingerie insiders say an everyday T-shirt bra should last only three to six months. Panties? Six months. Some people speculate that this short life expectancy is a form of conspiracy perpetrated by the apparel industry. Who cares what the reason is? I think the three-to-six-months rule is silly, an example of a consumerist mind-set that sees everything as disposable. Call me old-fashioned, but I try to make my lingerie last. Even though I have easy access to replacements, I don't throw out my bras and panties after just a few months, so why should you? The truth is, how long an item lasts really depends on how you treat it. If you put on that lace balconet bra only one time this year, it obviously doesn't need to be replaced quite so soon. Particularly if you keep it out of the washing machine. But look out for the signs that it might be time to move on, such as discoloration, loss of shape and elasticity, or torn, threadbare fabric.

CRACKING THE CODE

You might think of laundry as a simple (if tedious) task, but there are a lot of mistakes that can be made, particularly if you don't take a good look at the laundry care label on each garment. If you've never been able to decipher what all those hieroglyphics mean, here's a chart that translates these cryptic icons.

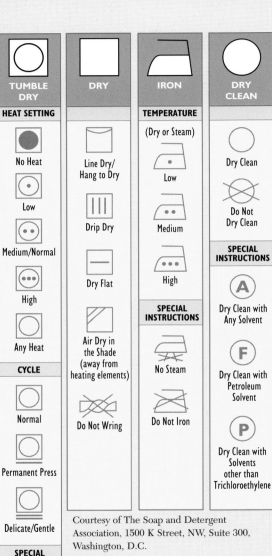

MACHINE WASH	BLEACH	TUMBLE DRY	DRY	IRON	DRY CLEAN
TEMPERATURE		**HEAT SETTING**		**TEMPERATURE**	
Cool/Cold	Any Bleach (when needed)	No Heat	Line Dry/ Hang to Dry	(Dry or Steam)	Dry Clean
Warm	Only Nonchlorine Bleach (when needed)	Low	Drip Dry	Low	Do Not Dry Clean
Hot	Do Not Bleach	Medium/Normal	Dry Flat	Medium	**SPECIAL INSTRUCTIONS**
CYCLE		High	Air Dry in the Shade (away from heating elements)	High	Dry Clean with Any Solvent
Normal		Any Heat	Do Not Wring	**SPECIAL INSTRUCTIONS**	Dry Clean with Petroleum Solvent
Permanent Press		**CYCLE**		No Steam	Dry Clean with Solvents other than Trichloroethylene
Delicate/Gentle		Normal		Do Not Iron	
SPECIAL INSTRUCTIONS		Permanent Press			
Do Not Wash		Delicate/Gentle			
Hand Wash		**SPECIAL INSTRUCTIONS**			
		Do Not Tumble Dry			

Courtesy of The Soap and Detergent Association, 1500 K Street, NW, Suite 300, Washington, D.C.

In Her Drawers

*N*ow that your lingerie's clean, it's time to store and organize it. If you're like most women, I'll bet your lingerie drawer resembles a tangled wad of straps stuck together like cold spaghetti left in the pot. It's enough to make you crazy . . . or think you are! Besides the pretty picture a drawer full of carefully arranged lingerie presents, you'll feel much more together if you know where to quickly find what you're looking for. It just takes a little time to set up a system that will make for much easier searches—no more last-minute panic attacks as you tear through your drawers looking for that perfect black strapless. A neat lingerie drawer is as much about sanity as vanity.

> **A neat lingerie drawer is as much about sanity as vanity.**

Before we begin, if you haven't yet disposed of anything that is worn out, stretched out, or has elastic popping out of it, kindly refer to our handy guide "Address Your State of Undress" (page 20) for lessons in dumping lingerie that has outstayed its welcome.

Getting dressed in the morning can be fun.

The way you organize your stuff really depends on your personal style—think about what you wear, how you get dressed, and what it is that slows you down when you're racing around trying to get out the door. The other factor is space—something nobody has enough of. If you can, give your lingerie a few drawers: one for bras and panties, and another for slips, shapers, hosiery, and other items you don't wear daily. Keep socks separate—they're like weeds and will spread out everywhere. In an ideal world, we'd all have plenty of room for proper storage, so think of space constraints as inspiration for your organizing.

1. **Separate.** Put bras, panties, and all other categories into their own piles. Further divide them into everyday and special-occasion items. In my own drawers, I separate thongs, boyshorts, and other panties into their own sections and bras into fancy and everyday. That's my system, but do whatever works for you. Some women organize by color, and then by style. Some keep bras and panties together for easier grabbing, while others separate them to divide and conquer.

Organize your bras and panties so that your everyday items are easily accessible. It might mean the pretty showcase pieces get pushed to the back, but you'll want those basic (but beloved) workhorses front and center. Separating your special-occasion items from your dailies also keeps them in better shape. You don't want your finest pieces constantly tossed around in the shuffle.

If you have the closet space, hang some of your larger items. Make sure they're hung well away from any hazards that might cause snags, and use notched hangers so straps don't slip, or padded hangers that won't crease or stretch delicate fabric. No one wants to end up with pointy, wire hanger–shaped shoulders on that special evening you decide to wear that cascading silk peignoir. Mommy Dearest would not approve!

2. **Think Inside the Box.** A great way to keep things organized is to use drawer dividers, or to store lingerie in pretty fabric- or tissue paper–lined boxes. For wood boxes and drawers, perfumed drawer liners help prevent fragile fibers from getting caught on rough spots—and offer a treat to the olfactory sense. Honeycomb-shaped sock organizers are actually also great for separating and storing thongs and panties, and can be used directly within a drawer or inside a box.

FINDING PEACE

*R*eaching into your underwear drawers is one of the first experiences you have each day. There's no need for it to be a struggle when you probably have other things to deal with—kids crying, work waiting, or just getting your hands on that first sip of morning coffee. Straightening out this one small corner of your life can give you a very rewarding sense of order, especially if the rest of your life feels like a similarly tangled web. Call it zen and the art of lingerie maintenance; you can improve your quality of life from the inside of your dresser drawers on out!

Store special-occasion items in lingerie bags (left). They're easy to travel with and totally versatile—use them to protect your pantyhose, stockings, and tights, too. Zippered plastic bags bags are particularly handy for organizing leg wear, which not only snags easily, but also can be very unruly—boa constrictors that wrap around everything they come into contact with.

3. **Make It Smell Sweet.** Don't forget about sachets. I love subtly scenting my little nothings. My personal preference is a warm, inviting vanilla scent. I use the same one at home that I sell in my store to create the legendary aroma that has made more than one man take a whiff and blissfully say, "I could die in here." If you're tempted, the signature La Petite Coquette sachets are sold in the shop and online at www.thelittleflirt.com.

Signature sachets make perfect scents.

4. **Know How to Fold 'Em.** Being told to fold your clothing may sound like something your mother would have said, but I'm here to tell you she was right. Here's a quick guide to maintaining order, even for the constantly busy slob (in all of us) who'd rather not be bothered. If you're gonna do it, do it right!

BRAS Close the hooks. Loose hooks get caught in fabric and lace and damage other bras. If space allows, spoon one bra into the other, cup into cup, creating a row that follows their natural curves. Spooning is particularly effective for contour bras because, if folded, one cup inevitably gets a permanent wrinkle from collapsing inward. Otherwise, after closing hooks, fold each bra in half, cup in cup, and line them up in columns like little soldiers.

PANTIES There's no secret industry method for folding panties. If you have the space, stack them like pancakes, one on top of the other. For a neat little square, fold in the sides and bring up the bottom. Or fold up the bottom and simply roll each one up. Here's where sock dividers make for an excellent storage option.

Lingerie Recovery

🌿 A Program for Change 🌿

If you've gotten to this point and realized, "Oh, no! I've been doing it all wrong," but aren't sure where to begin—don't worry. You needn't run out and buy everything all at once. It will take a while to build up the basics that will complete your collection. Think of it as a work in progress . . . and of me as your guide.

If you haven't parted with lingerie long past its prime, start now. (See "Address Your State of Undress," on page 20.) Until you do, we can't move ahead and start filling in the gaps. Lingerie is a personal matter, and so is the amount you choose to own. I suggest that, at minimum, you have enough everyday underwear to get you through two weeks without having to do laundry. Special occasions usually call for special outfits that, in turn, require special lingerie. Assess your collection of strappy, strapless, slinky, sheer, or just plain tricky clothing and buy the things needed to wear underneath. Every coquette also needs a few pick-me-up pieces, the beloved things that give the feeling that *this* is the day you've been waiting for.

First priority: **bras**—properly fitting ones. This is the most important of the life-changing, body-transforming, comfort-increasing purchases, so buy wisely. Either put yourself in the hands of a professional fitter or study this book and put what you've learned to the test. If a bra fits like a dream but its high price tag seems more like a nightmare, at least think about biting the bullet. The cost per wear will pay off in the long run, especially if you take good care of your purchase.

As you build your collection, shoot for owning seven comfortable bras; for versatility and a solid rotation, I suggest at least ten. For work and weekends, you should include some seamless ones that look smooth under blouses and T-shirts. Get a couple in black and a couple in nude. A shade that blends with your skin is more practical than white, because it is virtually invisible under light colors. A few colorful bras liven up the assortment and give your basics a break. A convertible bra that can be worn halter style, crisscross in the back, one-shoulder, or even backless is a good investment. A couple of racerback bras to wear under tank tops are essential. At least one strapless bra and a bustier/corset for both formal occasions and under tube tops and spaghetti-strap tanks will round out the bra wardrobe.

Beyond bras, it gets easier. **Camisoles are fundamental for their variety and versatility.** They can serve as liners under sheer tops and as pretty accents under blazers and cardigans. Choose from draping silk, simple cotton, or stretchy, control styles that smooth and shape. **For evenings and romantic encounters, look for pairs: a few beautiful, lacy, push-up bras in a variety of colors with matching thongs or other panties.** And, just for fun, splurge on at least one silk chemise or slip that hits your legs at midthigh.

Depending on your needs, you may want to invest in some shapewear for those bloated days and tricky outfits. Some basics with big rewards: control panties of any style or a body briefer for an all-over toned look.

The rules for panties are less specific. Some women buy matching bottoms for every bra and refuse to separate sets. If this sounds like you, get a couple of panties per bra, preferably in different styles. You should have some thongs to wear with tight pants, skirts, and clingy garments. Briefs of all shapes—from low-rise boyshorts to a high-cut leg with a fuller back—provide enough options to let you find the right underwear on any given day. Use the checklist at right to keep track of what you've got.

LIFE'S LITTLE LINGERIE LIST

*T*he following is a guide for a well-stocked lingerie wardrobe. Not everything included is a necessity—your choices depend on your personality and lifestyle. Check away!

Bras

- ☐ Seamless underwire
- ☐ Contour *(for under T-shirts)*
- ☐ Soft cup *(no underwire)*
- ☐ Padded or minimizer *(depending on your size)*
- ☐ Push-up or balconet *(for day/evening)*
- ☐ Convertible *(for halter, crisscross back, backless)*
- ☐ Strapless
- ☐ Sports
- ☐ Racerback *(for muscle Ts)*

Camisoles

- ☐ Basic *(plain lightweight for layering)*
- ☐ Control camisole *(for smoothing or shaping)*
- ☐ With built-in bra *(shelf or underwire)*
- ☐ Long *(to fill the space between shirts and low-slung pants)*
- ☐ Lacy *(for elegance and fun and sex appeal)*

Thongs

- ☐ Classic
- ☐ Low-rise
- ☐ G-string

Bikinis

- ☐ Classic
- ☐ Low-rise

Briefs

- ☐ Full coverage
- ☐ Boyshorts or hipsters
- ☐ High-cut leg

Shapewear

- ☐ Control briefs *(middle management, from stomach on south)*
- ☐ Body briefer *(all-over slimming)*
- ☐ Booty boosters *(rear lift and definition)*

Slips

- ☐ Full
- ☐ Half

Sleepwear

- ☐ Silk slip/chemise
- ☐ Comfy robe
- ☐ Slinky robe
- ☐ Gown
- ☐ Pajama set
- ☐ Babydoll

The Finishing Touches . . .

- ☐ Matching bra-and-panty sets
- ☐ Corset/bustier
- ☐ Waist cincher/waspie
- ☐ Garter belt and stockings
- ☐ Fishnets/seamed stockings
- ☐ Thigh highs
- ☐ Marabou or satin mules

Breast Friends

(Not for every day, but every once in a while)

- ☐ Adhesive bra *(for backless/ halter/strapless)*
- ☐ Silicone breast enhancers *(a.k.a. "chicken cutlets" or "outplants")*
- ☐ Breast petals *(to covers nipples when going braless)*
- ☐ Double-sided fashion tape *(to stick fabric to fabric or skin and stop slippage)*

Use Your Imagination . . .

(What would you like to have in your selection?)

- ☐ _____
- ☐ _____
- ☐ _____
- ☐ _____
- ☐ _____
- ☐ _____

The Fab in Fabric

*T*he material your lingerie is made of does more than make it look beautiful; it also determines how it feels next to your skin, how well it fits your body, and how long it will last. Here are some of the most common fabrics used in lingerie.

Chiffon WHAT IT IS: A sheer fabric made with a simple weave of tightly twisted crepe yarns. Originally made in silk, it is now also made in other fibers.

THE LINGERIE CONNECTION: A dreamy confection. Chiffon is delicate, diaphanous, and has lovely drape. A lighter and more revealing alternative to satin, it is often used for nighties, babydolls, camisoles, and robes *(left)*.

Cotton WHAT IT IS: A soft white vegetable fiber from the cotton plant that is composed mainly of cellulose.

THE LINGERIE CONNECTION: The comfort food of fabric *(right)*. Coming in many forms, from the finest combed cotton to fluffy terry, cotton is extremely comfort-

able, absorbent, durable, and washable. Beware of excessive shrinkage, though. Sometimes, taking a larger size is suggested for this reason. Don't be put off by a cotton blend—one with spandex stretches to make a garment even more comfortable to wear and helps the item retain its shape. No matter what material panties are made from, a cotton crotch lining is always recommended.

Elastic WHAT IT IS: A stretchable fiber, yarn, or tape generally made from natural or synthetic rubber (known as an elastomer). A synthetic, such as spandex, has all the stretch and recovery of natural rubber.

THE LINGERIE CONNECTION: Usually covered with another fiber, yarn, or fabric, elastic is found in a lot of lingerie—from bras that stretch to panty waistbands and legbands that "give." Elastic revolutionized intimates, but it's sensitive—any elasticized item should be air dried.

Georgette WHAT IT IS: Crepe woven both lengthwise and crosswise from twisted silk or polyester yarns to produce a dull yet delicately textured, grainy surface.

THE LINGERIE CONNECTION: Although opaque georgettes exist (and were popular in suits during the '80s), georgette for lingerie is usually sheer. The pebbly weave of georgette gives transparency but has slightly more coverage and weight than chiffon.

Microfiber WHAT IT IS: Made from manufactured filament fibers, it is spun out so that it is very thin, with virtually no grain when you run your hand along it (*above*).

THE LINGERIE CONNECTION: M is for miracle. Though synthetic, the fiber is lightweight, ultrafine, silky, and durable. Often blended with elastic, microfiber makes undergarments mold to the body so they move with you and bounce back to their original shape. Panties, bras, and camisoles in microfiber look supersmooth under clothing.

Nylon WHAT IT IS: Nylon, the first synthetic fabric ever created (1939), is composed of long chains of chemicals called polyamides.

THE LINGERIE CONNECTION: Garments made out of nylon generally have the light feel of silk except they are stronger, retain shape better, resist creases, mildew, and mold, and can be easier to care for than silk (almost always washable—and no water stains!). Often combined with spandex or other elastic fibers, nylon is used to make every form of lingerie. Because nylon is universally used in hosiery, the word *nylons* is now synonymous with pantyhose.

Polyester WHAT IT IS: Manufactured fibers made of acids and alcohols that come from petroleum. Introduced in the early 1950s, polyester is second only to cotton in worldwide use.

THE LINGERIE CONNECTION: Polyester is very popular in lingerie—it's strong, shape-retaining, easy to care for, and quick-drying. Higher-quality polyester and polyester blended with spandex or other fibers feel better next to the skin and fit the body well. Don't think about awful leisure wear from the '70s . . . today's polyester can feel fabulous.

Rayon **WHAT IT IS:** Man-made fibers produced from certain cotton fibers or wood chips. The name is derived from the French meaning "ray of light" because of its reflective quality.

THE LINGERIE CONNECTION: The fabric that democratized lingerie. With a luxurious silky feel, this fiber was called artificial silk, or "art silk," until 1927, when it was officially named rayon. Although Coco Chanel made a collection of gowns with this fabric in 1915, its widespread use was in less expensive versions of luxurious lingerie. It is shiny and lustrous, comfortable against the skin, absorbs dye well, and drapes nicely. Disadvantages include poor wrinkle recovery and a tendency to shrink.

Satin **WHAT IT IS:** Satin can refer to either a smooth, lustrous silk fabric woven with floating yarns (which reflect light) or the type of weave itself, which can be made of other fibers such as polyester or rayon. Sateen is cotton made in a satin weave.

THE LINGERIE CONNECTION: Soft and sensual, it feels like skin. The rich, glossy finish makes it a decadent fabric for all forms of lingerie—from robes and pajamas to camisoles, bras, and panties. Charmeuse is like satin, just shiny on one side, matte on the other—and luxurious on both sides. *(below)*

Silk **WHAT IT IS:** Silk is the fiber obtained from the cocoon of the silkworm.

THE LINGERIE CONNECTION: The queen of fabrics. Lustrous and lightweight, it drapes beautifully, feels sumptuous against the body, and accepts color dyes exceptionally well, making it the ultimate luxury in lingerie. Despite its delicate feel, silk is also known for its resiliency, elasticity, and strength. Stockings were originally made of silk before the advent of nylon, although silk versions are still available for those who can't wear man-made fibers or who simply seek the exquisiteness of the real thing.

Silk Knit **WHAT IT IS:** Silk fabric that is knitted rather than woven. It stretches and clings to the body.

THE LINGERIE CONNECTION: Soft, drapey, and surprisingly warm, silk knit is often used for thin layering pieces such as long underwear and camisoles. It provides warmth without bulk.

Spandex **WHAT IT IS:** Man-made fibers composed mainly of polyurethane.

THE LINGERIE CONNECTION: Stretch, strength, and shaping! Spandex is lightweight and provides garments with stretch and flexibility. Spandex is not used alone but blended with a variety of other fibers, such as nylon, polyester, silk, or cotton. It takes on many forms, from smooth and sleek fabric to stretch lace, is used in every type of lingerie, and gives the "shape" to shapewear. Lycra is a trademarked type of spandex.

Transformation Complete!

Does your bra feel better than anything you've worn before? Do you switch your lingerie like you change your outfits, depending on your mood and where the day is going to take you? Have you found a few little tricks that lure someone's eyes exactly where you want them to go? Do you open your lingerie drawer and see a delicious candy store selection to pull from? When you think of the many options of lingerie, isn't it hard to believe you didn't know all of this before? It's a whole new world under there. Look, we are crea-

> It takes a clean sweep to make you wonder, "Did I think I wasn't good enough for good underwear?"

tures of habit, and it can be hard to change our ways. If you're one of the people who thinks uncomfortable bras are a fact of life, it might take an experience with the right one to prove otherwise. But as you build your new life with lingerie and start to comprehend its power, it's impossible to turn back. When your panty drawer consists of pairs that are better unseen, it takes a clean sweep to make you wonder, "Did I think I wasn't good enough for good underwear?" If you're nervous about trying a lace teddy but get exactly the desired effect in a long satin slip, you understand lingerie's authority. Lingerie might be flimsy and frilly, but those delicates do pack a powerful punch. If you feel better, more sensual, and all-around more secure in yourself when you're walking around in silk panties, then you have been touched by the magic of La Petite Coquette. You are officially a little flirt!

Acknowledgments

A special thank you to Kenneth Kraeger for tearing off that first bra in a fit of passion, which ultimately lead to the birth of La Petite Coquette and my beautiful son, Daniel.

Enormous thanks to my collaborators:

Sarah Stark for her keen ear, who aptly captured the essence, sass and tone of my lingerie philosophy. What started out as weekend girly conversations at the beach can now be shared with you because she helped to refine years of my accumulated experiences and organized them into these pages.

Barbara Ladd, manager of my shop, personal assistant and resident know-it-all, who, from the moment we first met ten years ago, has believed in me and encouraged me to reach beyond my perceived limits in all endeavors, both professionally and personally. Her contributions, support, and rigorous editing were invaluable to the writing of this book.

Book agent, Carol Mann, who just happened into my shop. Had she not happily walked out wearing the best bra of her life, Workman would not have published this book.

I am so grateful for the time, talent, and tenacity of Susan Bolotin and Megan Nicolay, editors extraordinaire, and for the entire team at Workman, especially Janet Vicario, Ron Longe, Leora Kahn, Aaron Clendening, Sarah Norwood, Jill Wachter, and Munira Al-Khalili.

Much appreciation for:

My current "Coquettes" who help make my shop a New York City destination: Inna Vron, website manager of thelittleflirt.com; Naoko Nishizawa, merchandise manager), Jessica French, assistant buyer; Martina Solej, floor manager, senior associate, and resident photographer; Tania Garcia, senior associate; Lila Smith, associate; Elyse Rinaldi, associate; Denisha Navarro, merchandise assistant and associate.

Past "Coquettes," Karen Farrugia, Caroline Potterat Garson, Ania Golonka, Milagros Aquino, Nicole Meistrell, and all the others who helped me along the way.

Arthur Bruder, for making everything beautiful, and Cindi Sfinas for continuing in his path with stellar window displays.

Fay Greenspan, my mother, who instilled in me an appreciation for the finer things by passing on to me and my sisters the bedtime ritual of bathing in sweet scents and dressing in the most comfortable, dreamiest little nightgowns.

Harry Greenspan, my father, who gave me the spirit of salesmanship and swore I could "sell ice to Eskimos."

My sisters Esther and Sheri, brother Hal, grandfather Morris Greenspan, Tanta Leah, Uncle Henry Brystowski, Aunt Elizabeth, my mother-in-law in heaven, Mary Kraeger and the rest of my family whom I love.

All my friends: Pamela Korwin Wolf, Agnes Briley, Marlena Vendittuoli, Ingrid Drotman, Francesca Damato, Amy Ross, Doreen Gallo, Mary Ellen Kelly, Suzanne Stenger, andd Lisa Horowitz; trainers: Jonathan Espolin for his straight shooting about physical fitness and friendship, and James Bertrand who continues to train me to maintain my boundless energy and health; Freddie Rodriguez for always being on time, sharing laughter, and delivering me safely to my destinations; doctors: George Landberg for nurturing the child in me, Joel Kassimir for going beyond healing, Jon Snyder, John Bendo, Jeffrey Morrison, Keith Pyne, and Scott Kessler.

An enormous thank you to all the customers and vendors who supported me throughout the years and helped make La Petite Coquette what it is today, especially Fritz Humer, former big Kahuna at Wolford, Jennifer Puckett, George Abdelnour, Michael Rabinowitz, Leslie Wackerman, Akemi Gerber Stewart, David Reis, Suzanne Johnson, Olivia Feldman, Jeanette Edelstein, Tiziano De Franco, Ivana Nonnis, Connie Ancona, Gail Epstein, Leida Orzack, Krista Tonra, Melissa Schwartz, Bob Foster, John Festa, Andy Van Damme, Luis Fernandez, Araks Yeramyan, Christine Morton, Shirley Bobbins, Priamo, Leigh Bantivoglio, Sonia Winther, Mariela Rovito and Ali Meija, Ugo and Valeria Campello, Bubbles Smolev, Jean Luc Teinturier, Ben Yedder of Contours, and Dany Levy of Daily Candy.

To Jane Woolrich, whose feminine designs epitomize glamour, romance, and sensuality that continue to inspire me; and to Mark.

All the folks at QVC—Matt Guthartz, Joel Hanora, Jaime Lyn Ward, and Erin McLoughlin for recognizing what I have to offer women of all shapes and sizes.

Everyone at Carole Hochman—Seth Morris, Julie Moscatello, Donna Giambrone Ingram and Dina Ludovico—for making it happen.

Charles M. Green, whose inspired poem serves as the door to welcome you into my world of lingerie.

Bill Hoffman, for his business acumen and knowing how to talk to my heart and head at the same time.

Tom Morton, for simplifying my life by calmly lessening the burden of paying all those bills.

Larry Mattiasen for hooking me up to the twenty-first century with his technological expertise and further inspiring my creative spirit—and for "Dressing to Undress."